Robert Irwin

Robert Irwin

Exhibition organized by

Richard Koshalek
and
Kerry Brougher

With essays by

Robert Irwin

Sally Yard

John Hallmark Neff

Jeremy Gilbert-Rolfe

Klaus Kertess

Arthur C. Danto

Lawrence Weschler

Edited by

Russell Ferguson

The Museum of Contemporary Art, Los Angeles

Rizzoli International Publications, New York

This publication accompanies the exhibition "Robert Irwin," organized by
The Museum of Contemporary Art, Los Angeles,
and curated by Richard Koshalek and Kerry Brougher.

Presentation of "Robert Irwin" at MOCA is made possible in part by generous gifts from
The Henry Luce Foundation, Inc., Mr. and Mrs. Cleon T. Knapp and The Knapp Foundation.

Additional support has been provided by Max Palevsky, Count and Countess
Giuseppe Panza di Biumo, an anonymous donor, the Pasadena Art Alliance, and
the National Endowment for the Arts, a federal agency.

Exhibition Itinerary
June 20-August 15, 1993
The Museum of Contemporary Art, Los Angeles

March 15-May 15, 1994
Kölnischer Kunstverein

June 22-September 30, 1994
Musée d'Art Moderne de la Ville de Paris

January 31-April 17, 1995
Museo Nacional Centro de Arte Reina Sofía, Madrid

Editor: Russell Ferguson
Assistant Editor: Sherri Schottlaender
Design: Bethany Johns Design, New York
Printed by Typecraft, Inc., Pasadena

Library of Congress Cataloging-in-Publication Data
Irwin, Robert, 1928-
Robert Irwin / exhibition organized by Richard Koshalek and Kerry Brougher ;
with essays by Robert Irwin... [et al.] ; edited by Russell Ferguson.
      p.   cm.
Exhibition itinerary, June 20-August 15, 1993, the Museum of Contemporary Art
Los Angeles... and others.
      Includes bibliographical references.
      ISBN 0-914357-30-1 (MOCA)
      ISBN 0-8478-1770-9 (Rizzoli)
      1. Irwin, Robert, 1928-   —Exhibitions.   I. Ferguson, Russell.
      II. Museum of Contemporary Art (Los Angeles, Calif.)   III. Title.
N6537.I64A4 1993
709' .2—dc20   93-3337 CIP

Distributed by Rizzoli International Publications, Inc.
300 Park Avenue South
New York, New York 10010

Contents

Lenders to the Exhibition

Los Angeles County Museum of Art
The Museum of Contemporary Art, Los Angeles
Museum of Contemporary Art, San Diego
Norton Simon Museum, Pasadena
San Francisco Museum of Modern Art
Walker Art Center, Minneapolis

Mr. and Mrs. Donn Chappellet, St. Helena, California
Dr. and Mrs. Merle S. Glick, Los Angeles
Arne and Milly Glimcher, New York
Earl Lewis Goldberg, Brentwood, California
Estate of Helen Jacobs
Margo Leavin, Los Angeles
Richard and Frances Luban, Los Angeles
The Margulies Family Collection, Miami
Roberta Neiman, Los Angeles
Mr. and Mrs. Abraham Ratner, San Diego
Edward and Melinda Wortz, Pasadena
Anonymous lenders

871 Fine Art, San Francisco
Newspace, Los Angeles
The Pace Gallery, New York

Foreword and Acknowledgments

The Museum of Contemporary Art has long anticipated this opportunity to present a retrospective exhibition of the work of Robert Irwin. Yet such an effort, as Lawrence Weschler points out in this catalogue, "veritably basks in contradiction." For Irwin's journey as an artist, from his earliest Abstract Expressionist-inspired paintings to the site-determined environmental works of the last decade, is a logical, progressive deconstruction of art, a peeling away of the layers that had separated art from everything else. Irwin's quest has been no less than the total shift of art away from allusion and illusion to an art defined by experience, inextricably connected to the world yet by intentionality an entity solely unto itself. The very challenges associated with a retrospective of his work underscore Irwin's remarkable achievement.

The irony for museums is that over the years Irwin's work has become increasingly less "presentable," at least in a conventional sense. Irwin arrived on the scene at about the same time that painting, following the great moment of Abstract Expressionism in the late forties and early fifties, found itself in a cul-de-sac. Seemingly incapable of expanding theoretically or conceptually or of reducing itself any further for fear of ceasing to be, painting was limited to expanding physically, essentially magnifying the same moves that had already been made by the first generation Abstract Expressionists. Rather than remain trapped in a heritage that merely "illuminated what we have already come to know," Irwin began to ask questions about what a painting was; he began to see a painting not as a picture but as a physical object, and he began to identify and cast off its attributes one by one: as he searched for a means to reintroduce control, Irwin first aimed beyond monumental scale, then beyond representation and fictive space, then beyond the edge, and, ultimately and ever so logically, beyond painting itself—the complete rejection of the art object. From 1970 onward, Irwin found himself sitting outside art's self-contained, limited, but very functional systems for creation, presentation, and consumption—he found that he was no longer a "studio artist." From that point on Irwin set aside all assumptions of what art was, arriving at a type of work that was primarily installation or environmentally based, often temporal in nature, grounded in the frame of reference of the viewer, defined by perceptual phenomena, and determined by the unique circumstance of each site.

Whereas Irwin's early explorations could be comfortably represented in this retrospective, conveying the trajectory of his pursuits from 1970 onward was somewhat more problematic. Although much of the work could be documented with photographs—a means which has never been to the liking of the artist as it captures the image but not the "presence" of the piece—this seemed an inadequate solution in itself, though ultimately photographs were deemed necessary to provide a comprehensive overview of his many projects and proposals. Specific re-creations were out of the question as Irwin's work is determined by the distinctive conditions of spaces and sites, and cannot be properly re-created or re-experienced under different circumstances. The answer, it seemed, was for Irwin to create entirely new pieces, but in the spirit of previous work. For each stop on the exhibition tour, Irwin would create the most appropriate work for that space, recalling the scrim pieces from the seventies and early eighties with their almost alchemical transformation of light and space. Irwin's more recent site-determined works would be considered through a new piece realized for each institution in response to the site's characteristics and needs. As Irwin, over the last decade and a half, has shifted his art into an arena in which concepts and ideas are almost as important as the final product, his proposals for various unrealized projects had to be addressed as well. Presented in the exhibition is a full range of drawings and diagrams for Miami International Airport, a project that, despite the fact that it was never realized, remains one of Irwin's most ambitious and compelling works.

Clearly, such an exhibition called for a variety of creative efforts far beyond the ordinary on the part of all concerned. We must begin by thanking those individuals at the institutions participating in the tour who have been so sensitive to the special needs of the artist and exhibition. To Marianne Stockebrand, Director of the Kölnischer Kunstverein; Suzanne Pagé, Director, and Beatrice Parent, Curator, of the Musée d'Art Moderne de la Ville de Paris; and Maria de Corral, Director of the Museo Nacional Centro de Arte Reina Sofía in Madrid, we offer our utmost thanks for the time they have spent with Robert Irwin and the support they have provided for the realization of the installations and special projects at their respective institutions.

The conception and execution of this publication was the result of an unusually close and thoughtful collaboration between MOCA Associate Director Sherri Geldin, Editor Russell Ferguson, and Robert Irwin, along with Assistant Editor Sherri Schottlaender, all of whom rigorously explored various scenarios for creating the best possible book about Irwin's work. The successful results are clearly reflected in the essays included herein; we thank Sally Yard, John Hallmark Neff, Jeremy Gilbert-Rolfe, Klaus Kertess, Arthur C. Danto, and Lawrence Weschler for their insightful analyses of Irwin's work ranging from the late fifties to the present. Great appreciation is due designer Bethany Johns who, along with Georgie Stout, managed to produce a book that reflects Irwin's aspirations for a publication that would encourage its readers to think as well as to look.

The exhibition and tour required the talents of individuals from all departments at MOCA. From the start, Associate Director Sherri Geldin has participated in the conceptualization of the exhibition through countless twists and turns, and we are very thankful for her insights and expertise. John Bowsher, Exhibition Production Manager, worked closely with the artist to create a superb installation for all venues. We are also grateful to Exhibitions Coordinator Alma Ruiz for her skillful management of the exhibition budget and tour, and to Stacia Payne, first as a National Endowment for the Arts Curatorial Intern then as MOCA Curatorial Secretary, for her painstaking research of Irwin's works and for her enthusiastic assistance with all facets of the exhibition's organization. We are indebted to Jack Wiant, Chief

Financial Officer, for his everpresent financial counseling, and to Erica Clark, Director of Development, for her exceptional fundraising efforts. Chief Curator Paul Schimmel provided thoughtful support throughout the entire project, and, with Marilu Knode, assisted in the development of a preliminary checklist. Registrar Mo Shannon expertly coordinated the transportation of artworks, and Chief Preparator Eric Magnuson skillfully installed the work, from small, delicate paintings to complex installations. Sylvia Hohri, Assistant Director of Communications, and Dawn Setzer, Press Officer, planned and managed the public relations program. Director of Education Vas Prabhu, Associate Director of Education Kim Kanatani, and Art Talks Coordinator Caroline Blackburn developed and implemented the exhibition's educational components.

We would like to express our gratitude to Jack Brogan, who has worked closely with the artist over the years in the fabrication and conservation of many of his works, and to Leonard Feinstein, who provided the informative video for the exhibition. A special thanks is due Adele Irwin, who kindly and graciously provided us with the countless details needed for such an enterprise as well as often assuming the role of coordinator for various aspects of the project.

Presentation of "Robert Irwin" at MOCA is made possible in part by generous gifts from The Henry Luce Foundation, Inc., Mr. and Mrs. Cleon T. Knapp and The Knapp Foundation, Max Palevsky, Count and Countess Giuseppe Panza di Biumo, an anonymous donor, and the Pasadena Art Alliance; additional support has been provided by the National Endowment for the Arts, a federal agency. Without the generosity of these individuals and institutions, an undertaking of this scope could not have been realized, and we are grateful for their support. We are also most appreciative of the lenders to the exhibition, who have kindly agreed to part with their important pieces for the entire two year duration of the tour. Thanks also to Arne Glimcher, Marc Glimcher, and Renato Danese of The Pace Gallery, New York, and to Douglas Chrismas of Ace Contemporary Exhibitions, Los Angeles, for their ongoing encouragement and support of the exhibition.

Finally, this exhibition would not have been possible without the extraordinary vision and collaboration of Robert Irwin. We express our profound thanks to the artist not only for his commitment to this exhibition but also for his unparalleled early contribution to the founding of the museum itself. Above all, we thank him for his lifelong commitment to art, not just as one of the most significant artists of his time but as a teacher, mentor, and shaper of ideas and institutions.

MOCA's former Associate Director Sherri Geldin has collaborated with us in every aspect of the museum's development since becoming a member of Mayor Tom Bradley's Museum Advisory Committee in 1979. Given her keen and longstanding admiration for Irwin's work, it is especially fitting that her final contribution to MOCA was the crucial role she played in the realization of this retrospective. We dedicate this exhibition and its catalogue to her.

Richard Koshalek, Director   Kerry Brougher, Curator

Overleaf:

Source material for **Allée,** proposed 1990 (unrealized)

The Hidden Structures of Art

Robert Irwin

"Art is art-as-art

and everything else

is everything else."

—Ad Reinhardt

A Radical Art History

As students or artists we begin simply enough
with a blank canvas, and we don't think to ask ourselves:
what does that mean?

When we make a mark on that clean white expanse
and somehow magically it becomes a positive
in a sea of negative space, we don't ask ourselves:
how does that happen?

And when we compound our marks

into a variety of figurations—and see *in them* a variety of meanings,

we don't wonder to ourselves:

what does *that* mean?

Instead we simply accept this world of

compounded meanings, marks, and frame as given.

Or, at least, we could until we were confronted by a history as radical

as that of modern art's, and were made painfully aware

that such hidden orthodoxies are indeed open to question.

Jacques Louis David
The Coronation of
Napoleon and Josephine,
1805-07
Oil on canvas
240 1/8 x 366 1/2 inches
Musée du Louvre, Paris

When in the relatively short period of one century we could begin

with a pictorial reality so brilliantly conceived and executed as, say,

Jacques Louis David's *The Coronation of Napoleon and Josephine* (1805-07)

and within only a few generations find our world turned so upside-down

as to be confronted by the stark reality

of Kasimir Malevich's *Suprematist Composition: White on White* (1918)

and challenged by his declaration that this "desert" of a canvas

was in fact "a world of pure feeling,"

then such seemingly abstract and fruitless questions as those asked above

become quite relevant.

Kasimir Malevich
Suprematist Composition:
White on White, 1918
Oil on canvas
31 1/4 x 31 1/4 inches
The Museum of Modern Art,
New York

This history is neither accidental nor incidental.

 It is an almost methodical step-by-step de-structuring

of those logics underwriting a pictorial reality—

hIerarchies of meanings as once ordered by transcendent beliefs

or singular concepts of truth and social order.

Willem de Kooning
Easter Monday, 1955-56
Oil and newspaper transfer on canvas
96 x 74 inches
The Metropolitan Museum
of Art, New York
Rogers Fund, 1956

In Western thought it has become embedded in each of us

to first search out the quantitative in everything—

without fully realizing that in the headlong pursuit of such practicalities

we have inevitably developed a resistance

to all that is ineffable in experience.

Show us an Abstract Expressionist painting and we quickly ask:

what is it? or what does it mean?

Questions which in effect say: take this thing, which is right in front of me—

and let me understand it, not by experiencing it, but by referencing it away from its

immediate presence to whatever it is we assume it is intended to re-present.

Making it once again into a duality of abstraction, vis-à-vis the singularity,

"it is," it was declared to be by the artists.

To this day most of us still try to Rorschach or psychoanalyze these works of art.

The problem here is not a matter of there being anything wrong

with "practical" thinking per se,

but more a question of our misapplying the usefulness of its logics

outside their area of competence.

I mean if I ask you, "How many homeless people does $E=mc^2$ house?"

and the answer is none, can I conclude from this that $E=mc^2$ is meaningless,

or have I simply asked the wrong question?

Modern art's seeming "impracticality" was and still is misconstrued

in the view of many as art's having lost its way.

On the contrary, the degree of art's estrangement from such seeming "norms"

is in fact an actual measurement of the depth of implied change, not only in art,

but in art's implications for radical social change—

beginning with the fundamental problem: you can't get there from here.

To assume that everything can and should reveal itself

in terms you are already familiar with

is the hallmark of conventional thinking.

But to require that B reveal itself in terms of A

is to negate the very meaning of B in itself.

That we both think and feel,

and that they are fundamentally different,

is self-evident.

This relationship is not some thesis met by an anti-thesis in an intellectual vacuum.

It is a complex, real-time intersection

of equally necessary complements—

the conditional resolution of which is in the process

of my continuously reasoning—making whole—my actually being in the world.

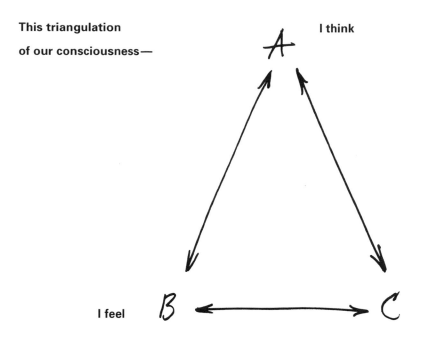

This triangulation
of our consciousness—

I think

I feel

the particular circumstances
within which and for which
I find myself at every moment

—is the dynamic of our being phenomenally in the world as an active participant
in its becoming real for us. This is the nexus of modern thought.
That we make and remake (choose) our own reality (at least in part)
may well be the only truly creative human action.

The Hidden Orthodoxy of Pictorial Logic

The idea of questioning something so fundamental as our own grasp on "reality"
is to say the least a tricky one.
To start with, we don't have an actual place to begin at the beginning.
We are, of course, immersed in this world as we have already come to know it—
our own orthodoxies neatly hidden behind the obvious—i.e., what it is
we think we already know.

Take the case in point—the orthodoxy of the frame and mark
as somehow a given in art. One look around tells us there are no such frames
in our perception of the world. And as to the marks we make on our canvas,
they acquire their special *significance* by virtue of being seen as intended—
as opposed to something accidental or found, a scratch or a blemish.
This significance has the power to raise our marks out of—above—
their incidental surroundings, thereby establishing
the fundamental figure/ground relationship that underwrites
the highly stylized learned logic of pictorial perception.

The Coronation of Napoleon and Josephine provides us with a classic illustration
of the consequences of this concept of "figure and ground" carried to its extreme—
of how in pictorial art an abstract hierarchy of mark, frame, and meaning
content translates structurally as deep pictorial space
with carefully meaning-structured strata of composition.

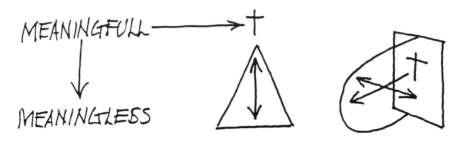

Once such a meaning structure is clearly in place
it will come to further condition *what* as well as *how* we see.
This meaningful/meaningless hierarchy of figure/ground, positive/negative ordering
will carry over to affect our sense of thing and non-thing, real and unreal,
and finally even to determine what is seen and not seen.
Such a learned logic, once in place, will condition our perception to simply omit
that which has been pre-determined to have no real meaning-content.
Of course we all think we simply see, and in a manner of speaking we do—
but do we really? How many times have you forgotten your keys
and had to go back into the house to find them?
But with your mind still preoccupied you can look straight at your keys
and still not see them. In this same sense (our perception tied up with attending)
we pass through the world habituating and editing out
much more than we ever acknowledge.
These are not simply idle games we play on Sundays at the art museum.
Seeing is the initial act of valuing, and the nature and infinite potential
of human beings to see and to aesthetically order the world
is the *one pure subject of art*.

Consider now for a moment the implications

of Malevich's *Suprematist Composition: White on White*.

Besides representing the culmination of the nineteenth-century process

of devaluing the meaning/content of the pictorial "mark,"

it exhibits the results of the corresponding physical and structural changes

that led to the space of painting becoming increasingly shallow,

now to be virtually flat, paint and surface becoming increasingly physical,

the relationship of edges—how things meet and touch each other—

now even more palpable and telling, color and scale both real and first hand.

Structurally, the import is in the flattening of the traditional hierarchy

of ordering relationships.

Now what if we were to take all of this—the implications of the changes

in nineteenth-century art and the conditions of Malevich's art—

seriously? (But then how else do we actually value something?) What then?

A mark with no meaning? A painting space with only the particulars of paint,

and no ordering devices to aid us in understanding what we see?

How do we live with that?

A Non-Hierarchical Order

No artists worth their salt have ever tried to make their art abstract—as in obscure.

Artists have always tried to make their art as real as is humanly possible.

What is at stake here is what we mean by the term *real.*

The populist argument against modernism has always centered on

the loss of the beloved figure to modernism's so-called "abstractions."

The mistake in this kind of thinking is in treating humanism and the human figure

as one and the same. On the contrary, in this shift in form

something more profound than a simple shift in style has taken place.

The abstract sign, human-figure, has been replaced

by an expanded responsibility for the individual artist/observer

as actively charged with completing the *full intent* of the work of art—

experientially.

To compound this argument:

in art the term *humanism* is most critically linked

with the difficult concept of creativity—

an idea which means absolutely nothing

if in fact the individual does not, at least in part,

act directly in setting in motion his or her own meaning.

It is precisely here, in raising up the level of self-determination,

that the artists of the nineteenth and twentieth centuries

so distinguished the art of the present from the art of the past

that an unprecedented need for an extended definition for art—modern—

was required. This transference of responsibility

to the individual observer to complete the work of art

is the implicit meaning integral to so-called abstraction.

At the heart of this modernism

is a new concept of time and determined relations as being continuous

rather than incremental, inclusive rather than exclusive.

Where the qualities and duration of phenomenal perception

are fully extended in an interactive state of flux,

never fully predictable, and never fully resolved, and *may* exist only as long

as the individual perceiver keeps them in play.

In this sense, practicing phenomenal perception

is the equivalent of practicing in the fourth dimension.

The Myth of the Art World

In the short term view the overwhelming illusion

is that the "art world" makes it all up for us.

That curators, critics, dealers, patrons, and historians determine what art is.

While it is true that all of these players have a role to play,

in the long term it is artists who distill what is art,

and they do so by the commitments they make *as* artists in their work.

A splendid example of this myth is the illusion

that the "color field" painting of the sixties was important art.

Certainly by all of the short-term measures—

visibility, critical acceptance, economics, etc.—

you had to think its place in art history was assured.

These were virtuoso performances,

coming directly on the heels of Abstract Expressionism,

fueled by one of its most respected critics, underwritten by influential curators,

and sold to most every important art collector and museum

as virtually essential to a modern collection.

And yet, not thirty years have passed and the whole impressive enterprise

has died from its own lack of weight: pure performance with no real consequences.

Finally, there were no real questions in "color field" painting

to challenge a new generation of artists.

What is equally fascinating about this recent art world phenomenon

is how easily the supposedly sophisticated art world community

was seduced by a literary sleight of hand and a pretty picture

into thinking that pictorial flatness was a real issue in the late twentieth century.

Physical flatness!

When all around us in every other discipline—physics, sociology, mathematics—

everyone else was wrestling with such multi-dimensional concepts

as chaos theory and ethno-methodology, quarks and black holes,

fractals and rubber sheet geometry!

No, where such fundamental questions are concerned,

the world is just not that out of balance.

The "formalism" of pictorial flatness was a red herring which failed altogether

to address the multi-dimensional questions of a generation of artists

potentially freed from the limitations of a pictorial logic.

The real issues in modern art's dramatic structural shift from the illusion

of deep pictorial space to a space of interlocking figure and ground,

and then to an art of extended dimensions are in the flattening of hierarchy

in determining order and meaning. The questions for an art

of extended dimensions should be: What would a non-hierarchical order look like?

What would be its operative (extended) frame of reference?

How might it work?

And what kind of a world would it make?

Keep in mind that,

1)

We do not invent our consciousness.

Here attending is the equal of discovery,

since by the time we can conceive of a change

the grounds for it are already in us.

This is the genius of Husserl's phenomenal ground, Malevich's pure desert,

and Reinhardt's art-as-art, as a designating place in our individual consciousness

where we can get in touch with, raise up, and re-evaluate

those tacit dimensions which already course through our lives.

2)

Our discoveries do not, and should not,

go directly into the world of our collective lives.

They must first necessarily undergo the various processes

of *discipline* and social *innovation*.

Overleaf:
Source material for
Two Architectural Towers,
proposed 1989 (unrealized)
City Front Plaza, Chicago

Art as a Discipline

What I would like to do now is take our familiar structural hierarchy,

remove its *transcendent concepts*

(with the intent of replacing them with a single *infinite subject*),

and to in effect turn it on its side and begin to think of all our art world actions

as part of our everyday process of social innovation.

One responsible for the recognition, maturation, and development into practice

of our individual creative actions.

What were earlier hierarchically characterized as rungs on a ladder

in an upward progression should now be thought of as interlocking—equal value—

art actions that *collectively* go to make the discipline

of art into meaningful social action.

(This concept of art as a discipline can effectively exist

either as a formal or tacit relationship.

All that is required is a shared sense among the principals

as to the nature of the pure subject

and a shared need to pursue its consequences.)

As a result of the various dialogues of modernism,

the alternative to a hierarchical ordering is already in us,

and is already a tacit dimension of our practices.

What we need to identify is how, and on what grounds,

this non-hierarchical dimension works.

The Pure Subject of Art

What is the unique contribution of art that justifies its lofty social position?

Can we continue the practice of simply enlisting art as illustrator or apologist

for every other kind of social or political cause?

Or does Art have a meaning of its own?

And if not, how do we then continue to call it a creative action?

And don't we then value it too highly?

Certainly the word "Art" has come to signify so many things

that it no longer effectively signifies anything.

It has become a particularly confusing *objective* fixation

to mix up the *objects* of art, with the *subject*—"art."

This leads us to mistakenly begin our inquiries with the objects as the subject.

Instead of acting as a useful descriptive term that speaks to a real performance

or purpose, "Art" has become a kind of honorarium for good behavior.

So if we are to try and identify a pure subject of art,

we will first need to take back the subject from its various objects.

This fixation has been compounded for us

both by our *objectively* structured histories

(the biases in the way we make up our histories)

and the educational habit of introducing each of us *to* art by way of its objects

with only an occasionally vague reference to those root questions *from* which

each art object emerges as only one speculative answer—

which is like expecting water to run uphill.

As for our concept of historymaking, it lacks either the insight or a method to

recognize and value the quality of our *questions* at the moment of their inception.

(Which is why all of our so-called "renaissances" are placed at the end of each

epoch as a quantitative measure of performance.) When, as we know,

answers are the direct result of properly posited questions.

The one exception may be the unique moment of Russian Constructivism,

where in a few explosively creative years, with the level of performance limited,

often even crude, artists were able to formulate extended questions

that still stimulate and inform contemporary art.

Art as a pure subject is a *non-thing.* That is, it has no actual physical dimensions

or, if you wish, infinite physical dimensions.

This art exists in the pure void of concept, and as such it is the infinite potential

from which all our art actions are drawn.

The term "pure" is not being used as a value judgment

or as some kind of mystification. It is simply intended as a descriptive word

to indicate such things as the open potential of our perception,

or the sheer complexity of the world, which must for all intents and purposes

be viewed as infinite.

The Art of Pure Inquiry

The art of pure inquiry is an open interface between the pure subject—
all that is out there—and the pure potential of the individual perceiver—
all that is in here. Where the strength (clarity) of this inquiry lies
is in its single motive—*the desire to know.*
While the aspiration for a transcendent art is a beautiful idea,
the changing history of art makes it quite clear we have not achieved
any such transcendence. So while each new generation of artists
can be seen as having produced an art which may be a perfect representation
of their unique moment in time and place,
and while it is true that each of these arts is art, it is equally true
that none of these arts is *art* per se. As magnificent as each of these arts may be,
it is by now quite obvious that none of them has ever managed
to subsume the subject. A fact which requires that each new generation of artists
begin at the beginning:
with a *pure* inquiry into the *pure* subject.

As artists, the one true inquiry of art as a pure subject
is an inquiry of our potential to know the world around us
and our actively being in it, with a particular emphasis on the aesthetic.
This world is not just somehow given to us whole.
We perceive, we shape the world, and as artists we discover and give value
to our human potential to "see" the infinite richness (beauty?) in everything,
creating an extended aesthetic reality.

That we attend and act on this ever-changing aesthetic richness
is the single thread that ties all of the arts, past and present, into one art intention.
That we intend the world for ourselves and set in motion
our own unique values—reality—meaning,
is the one true creative human action.

Pure Motive / Pure Method

Certainly the pure void of concept beckons the curious.

The unique motive for a pure inquiry of a pure subject is curiosity,
the desire to know. This curiosity is the single motive
which takes us in the opposite direction
from all of our other "normal" collective social drives.

Our posture (method) is that of philosophies—wonder, with its special ability
to set aside, for the moment, the practical for the purely speculative.
Pure wonder is that special state of mind—of enthusiasm and appreciation—
that gives us the balance for such an ephemeral inquiry into the pure potential
of our lives. First, because it gives us the means to suspend judgment,
and second, because it does not require closure.

The Art of Colleagueship

It is shared curiosity that ties individual creative actions into a dialogue
of immanence. A special feature of which is the willingness
of the participants to temporarily suspend judgment
so as to seriously entertain the open potential of our discoveries.

That nothing occurs in a vacuum is an idea which is particularly true
of human actions. So while the art of pure inquiry is uniquely individual,
it does not take place in isolation. Now think back to our earlier argument
that each new generation of artists makes an art which can be said to be
a perfect representation of their moment in time and place.
What is key here is that certain ideas (possibilities) are immanent
at particular moments. That in each time and place there exists
a unique body of shared experiences, knowledge, and need,
that marks our moment in time, and from which all inquiry steps off.
(Merleau-Ponty, in writing about the work of Cézanne,
reflected that art may have an advantage over philosophy as
a speculative thought form in that it has at once a tactile and a cerebral dimension.)

In this sense no one is ever really ahead of their time.
If I can think something it is because it has become ripe for thinking,
and it is only reasonable to suppose that someone else is sharing my thoughts.
Although it may seem little solace for what can often feel
like a lonely and unconnected life, we are never fully alone in our thoughts.
Instead anyone actively seeking out the potential of their moment
is having a dialogue of colleagueship, and it is in this way
that we *collectively* begin to define the art of our own time.

Art as Art

Our new ideas, no matter how right we may think they are,

do not go into the world of our collective lives ad hoc,

where they might cause chaos. Unlike informal exchanges with our colleagues,

where we may willingly suspend judgment and openly speculate

with little evidence, art as art requires that a process of testing, maturation,

and judgment be applied to the potential of each of our new discoveries,

weighed with and against the existing body of knowledge and practice.

What had up till now been open speculation now takes on the character

of organized exhibition and publication. For the participants,

this is the beginning of a more formal exchange of ideas.

Exhibition, which begins as an active give and take dialogue among the principals,

features on one hand the difficult transformation (in all dimensions)

of what was previously known otherwise, (in feelings or thought)

into an inter-subjectively available form (a work of art?), with properties

which can be weighed as evidence of the proposition(s) in question.

On the other hand, it begins the social process of questioning why

and to what end we should modify our existing body of knowledge

or any of our accepted beliefs and practices to accommodate the added dimensions

of any such new propositions.

For example, while in the beginning the preponderance of evidence

weighed heavily against Einstein's speculative proposition $E=mc^2$,

it was seriously entertained by a few, mainly because of its aesthetic beauty

and potential as an idea. But such acceptance brings with it

a large responsibility to supply the proof.

Someone must now make the commitment of time, resources, and reputation

to establish, for example, whether a light ray

really does bend around a gravity field.

The point is that we don't just abandon what works for a pretty idea

until much of our in-house (art as art or science as science) homework is done.

In due time this discipline of our individual discoveries will broaden out

into ever expanding areas of social innovation,

where a whole range of added social (collective) motives will come into play.

Art as Social Action

If our discovery had been electricity

and we had exhibited a light bulb

we would now set out to light up the city,

with all of its attendant consequences and benefits,

and the social consequences of our actions would be

a measure of their meaning.

Our simple motive, the desire to know,

is now joined by the more complex motive, the need to effect.

Our individual meaning is now joined by another kind of meaning assignment,

giving us a compounded (two kinds of) motive and meaning.

I should add that lighting up the city

no more exhausts the potential in the discovery of electricity than, say,

David's *The Coronation of Napoleon and Josephine* exhausts perspective.

Which is why subsequent generations of artists may continue to focus on

and legitimately develop the consequences of any single discovery.

Let me add that the success or failure of any idea at this level can vary

from culture to culture dependent on any number of social variables

having no direct bearing on the quality of the ideas *per se*.

Earlier we asked whether art could continue to act as an illustrator or apologist

for social or political causes. The answer is no.

"Art" developed in this manner—acting on/acting out abstract concepts

of social or political "good"—is first and foremost just that,

an illustration of those abstract concepts.

First we change, and then we change our practices, and only later do we think

to collectively change our institutions—to bring them in line with

who we have become. It is in this context that we understand

that change causes revolutions, rather than, as is usually supposed,

revolutions causing change.

For art to have any intrinsic social meaning

it needs to be developed from a subject of its own.

Art capable of real social meaning—change—

is art capable of manifesting a new set of values.

New perceptions breed new values. They breed them tacitly, by implication.

We do not as a social body choose explicitly a new set of values.

Instead we submit to them by the very act of dwelling in them:

first by creating them, and then in the process of adapting them

through practices that can clearly be seen to enhance our lives.

It is in this way, from the ground up, and not administered from the top down,

that art most creatively affects the quality of our social good.

The Practice of Art

The practice of art is where we begin to weave the richness of our perceptions,
now grounded in particular social actions, into the very fabric of our daily lives.

Practice has from the start a practical side to it,
performance as opposed to speculation or activism—
to give practical expression to, and finally to follow as a way of life.
Our aesthetic values exhibited as art inform and ground
our collective sense of beauty, order, style, taste, fashion, etc.,
providing a standard for those working examples of "aesthetic" application
to an ever-increasing range of social practices.
More covertly, but with equal importance, this aesthetic understanding
also bears directly on all of our attempts to plan, order, shape, form, etc.,
and to the building of all of our various social organizations and institutions.
It is this deep seeding of our values into the very fabric of our everyday lives
that results in what we mean by our use of the term *culture*.

The tendency to question the seriousness of all these art practices
is a key flaw in all hierarchical thinking. It fosters the negative habit
of turning our conversation about art into confrontations for art:
arguments calculated to capture for one position or another
the *bauble* of high art—in place of a more substantive dialogue
as to the what and why of art.
If, for example, a particular view of art, such as the "formalism of flatness," or
a "conceptualism" that pronounces "painting is dead," or a politicizing of art
to deny its aestheticism, should hold sway as a momentary definition for art,
as has happened, then everything else is, by degrees, cast down as less than art.
Which in effect forces everyone to scramble around spending lots of energy
in games of social confrontation, as does take place,
intended to dethrone the obvious limitations such views place on the whole of art.
Worse yet, such confrontations are seldom intended to open up the dialogue,
so much as replace somebody else's dogma with our own brand of dogma.

From a non-hierarchical perspective, the discipline of art as a process
of social innovation has a distinctly different character.
So long as each of these actions, art as pure inquiry, art as social action,
practice, etc., contributes something unique
(accomplishes something each of the others does not)
to the overall process of art's social innovation,
then you cannot correctly say that one art action (motive)
is more real or important than another.
Unless you can fully subsume one art action to the other
they must be considered equal in value.

This is not to say that individuals cannot and do not participate

in the innovation of their own ideas, cannot choose to move from one art action

to another; it is to say that each action has a separate and distinct motive and role.

For example: Einstein took the time to write a primer on his theory of relativity.

Here the intent was not to extend his personal knowledge, but to communicate,

to share his ideas. For us to intend something

requires not only a commitment of our time and energy,

but a particular state of mind.

To help clarify this point, let me state an organizing principle

for the concept of a non-hierarchical ordering by paraphrasing Ad Reinhardt's

"art is art-as-art and everything else is everything else"—that something is—

whatever it is that makes the principal decisions in its becoming what it is.

Since everything exists on more than one level, and can be understood, in part,

from more than one perspective, to know what something fundamentally is

we need a more specific context within which we can make our determinations.

This is especially true when we are dealing with subjects as ambiguous as art

and as ambitious as creativity, where the working decisions of its becoming

are what it is all about. To do this we need to triangulate our inquiries by

factoring in our individual intentions, i.e. what it is we want or need to know or do.

With this joining of intention with the pure subject and the existing body

of knowledge and practice we gain the specific context with and against which

we can weigh the relative value of each of the particulars of our creative actions.

Art as Historical Form

Art history acts as the keeper of the flame for the whole of art as a discipline,

charged with the responsibility to carefully choose and mull over

those most meaningful art actions as measures both of the creative impulse

and its social implications.

Memory is the active model for both the character and role of history in our affairs.

Our memory is multi-faceted, having literally many kinds, levels, and durations,

all necessary to accommodate the complexity of actions that go to make up the

whole of our individual and collective consciousnesses.

As with memory, there are any number of individual and collective histories.

Art as historical form is a general history made up of numerous individual histories,

within a set of other discipline histories, that collectively form a subset

within an overall social history.

History, like memory, is selective.

History is not so much a measure of the quality of our discoveries or ideas

(electricity or the light bulb *per se*) but more a measure of their social, political,

and cultural effect (the result of lighting up the city).

In seeking to discern and assign values and meanings, history begins

by looking for the consistencies and historical overlaps in our various art actions,

producing a distinctly quantitative bias.

On the other hand this history in effect balances out the more eccentric

(pure inquiry begins with the inconsistencies) values

assigned to our actions as individuals and the kinds of activist meanings

we give to our social and political actions.

While, as we have stated earlier, artists determine what art is,

this action cuts two ways. Artists set in motion their own meaning,

but art is always at least in part in response to art.

By acting on the legacy of questions (potential) inherent in the art

of their predecessors, they raise up and shed new light on this history of art.

At the same time historians as activist/critics participate directly

as the representatives of the existing body of knowledge in a give and take process

of weighing the worth of the new perceptions of artists

with and against what we already know and value.

We have now identified at least three kinds of art meaning—

individual, social/political, and historical—

each with its own particular kind of correctness and import.

Have we now arrived at the threshold of Mondrian's

"culture of determined relations?"

Certainly meaning as having more than one source, more than one reality

(i.e. non-hierarchical) needs to now be considered as *conditional*.

Let me give the briefest of examples

for how such contextual frames of reference actually work.

Picture our practitioner as a bridge builder, whose activities occur in the areas

of social action and practice. The act of building a bridge is triangulated

by our *intention*—the desire/need to build the bridge, the *potential*—

how the bridge might be built, and the *history*—how bridges have been built

up till now. We don't build bridges on speculation they just might fall down—

at the same time we don't simply repeat how bridges have been built.

The state of the art of bridge building lies at the apex of that *moment*

formed between the need, occasion, and circumstances for the bridge—

the potential for building a bridge—and the history of bridge building.

Within this framework the practitioner has the context for determining

all of the particulars, both physically and aesthetically, for the bridge.

While at the same time we the user, critic, historian, aspiring bridge builder

can evaluate the bridge in the act of driving over it and having access

to the same information that initially informed the building of the bridge.

As I have laid it out, art is pure inquiry, colleagueship, art as art,

art as social action, practice, and historical form.

Each a context within a set of contexts, each a specific intention put in play

by individual practitioners holding a collective art aspiration.

Individually and together they form a discipline of art.

A compound of operative frames of reference for the orderly innovation—

discovery-to-practice—of art.

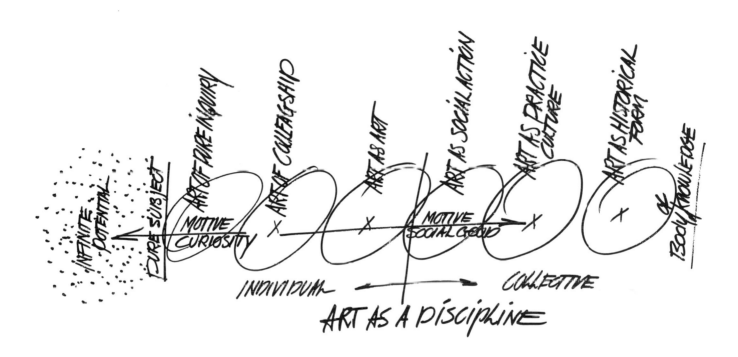

Overleaf:
Sentinel Plaza, 1990
Pasadena Police Department, Pasadena, California
(detail of painted wall)

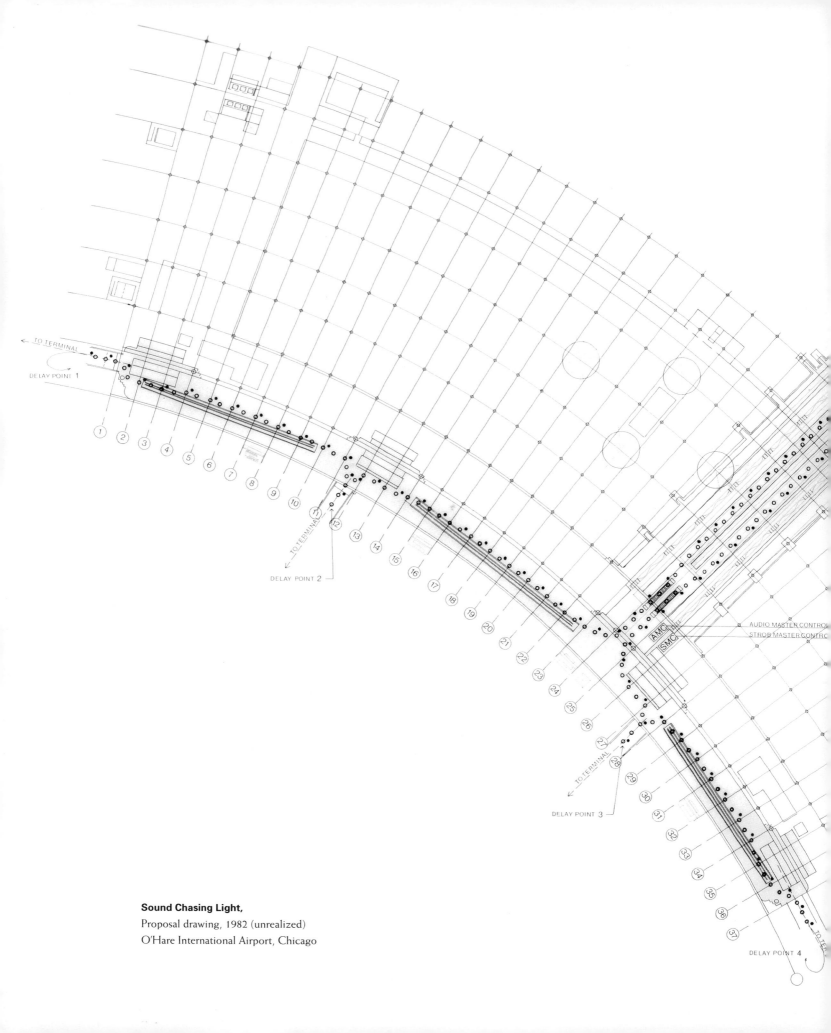

Sound Chasing Light,
Proposal drawing, 1982 (unrealized)
O'Hare International Airport, Chicago

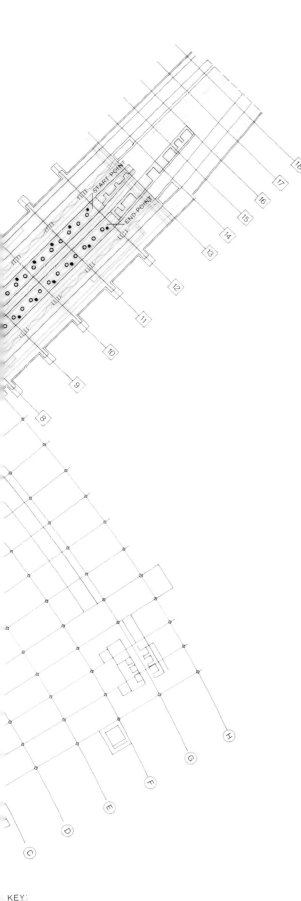

Deep Time

Sally Yard

Arriving via Chicago's rapid transit train, the traveler undertakes a lengthy interior walk to reach the O'Hare Airport terminals. Pressing onward, suitcase in tow, the viewer suddenly senses a flash of light racing ahead. Gone as swiftly as it appeared, it was perhaps imagined, or a power surge, some refraction of the airstrip lights beyond. A moment later a cello's low G and A are discerned amidst the din. The longing tones emerge as a sonorous image of swift movement, disappearing around the corner and into the distance as if in pursuit of the ephemeral luminosity. Alerted, the pedestrian moves along, the mirage of light and sound, the illusion of chase, subsiding into the hustle to catch a plane, to meet a flight. When suddenly the light shoots by again, confirmed now, real. And on its heels, the slow-bowed sound.

Sound Chasing Light would scarcely make sense anyplace or anytime but in that long walk from the city's subway link. The work in fact was never realized, confounded by an intractable contractor.[1] Composed of energies rather than images, it was to cut through the tedium of this twentieth-century passage stripped of the ceremonies of arrival and departure. And it was funny, abstractly, like a score for a Buster Keaton chase scene.

Sleek though the line of light would have been, affecting as the chord might have sounded, these were agents, not objects, in Robert Irwin's attenuation of attention, contradiction of habituation. Twice, maybe three times, caught unawares, the mobile inhabitants of the late twentieth century would be ready, watchful, the numbing duration jostled by curiosity into consciousness. And in this urban juncture the parameters of space and time within which all of our experience unfolds would be made articulate.

KEY:
STROBE FIXTURES 14'0" ON CENTER
AUDIO FIXTURES 28'0" ON CENTER

Early in the 1950s, in the heyday of Abstract Expressionism, Tony Smith took a drive one night on the New Jersey Turnpike, still under construction. "I thought to myself, it ought to be clear that's the end of art. Most painting looks pretty pictorial after that. There is no way you can frame it, you just have to experience it."[2] Smith himself, trained as an architect, crony of the Abstract Expressionist painters, and, by 1962, proto-Minimalist sculptor, continued to make paintings and objects. But in 1967 *Smoke*, composed of black-painted wooden forms, expanded to fill the breadth of the Corcoran Gallery's two-story atrium space, its outer dimensions, if not its inner, crystalline structure, determined by context.[3] Smith of course hadn't conceded "the end of art" in his own life. But he had apparently—as Michael Fried detected with dismay, and as Hal Foster later enunciated with precision—foreseen the crux that separates Clement Greenberg's modernism from the "expanded field" of Minimalism.[4] On that desolate but exhilarating highway—about as low as one could get in terms of formalist art— Smith sensed the rift in intention and practice between art that is self-contained—inside the boundaries of medium and within the edges dividing art space and our space—and an art which engages the world and the viewer.

Tony Smith
Smoke, 1967
Wood
24 x 31 x 48 feet
Installation at the Corcoran Gallery, Washington, D.C.

Irwin probably hadn't heard the story in the fifties, and in any case was unlikely to embark on radical change in his own life based on someone else's revelations. Not that the muscular force of the freeway was lost on him. He grew up in Los Angeles, after all, and invested his first major earnings in a 1930s roadster. It was not the bleak languor of Joan Didion's "life styles in the golden land"[5] that Irwin felt, but instead the lightness of a city short on time past, thick with time present.

In this city that was, in art as in life, relatively unencumbered with tradition, Irwin would eventually reach a broader understanding of art than either painting or sculpture could afford. Art operates, for Irwin, as a form of thought; thought, like form, should be bare of extraneous detail. Having in the sixties distilled painting to a nearly irreducible state, Irwin turned in the seventies to the vaporous surround. This elemental envelope rendered lucid if persistently ineffable, in the eighties Irwin ventured into the less rarified realm of the city, the campus, the garden, the atrium, the airport. From painting to freeway portal, the process had to do with cutting through layers of "compounded abstraction" to locate underlying motives, to identify fundamental conditions. All of this, however, had little to do with pinpointing anything absolute or timeless.

By the late sixties two things were certain for Irwin: change is constant; everything exists in relationship. On one level these paired principles of flux and relativity were inescapable twentieth-century intuitions. Yet how exactly they are incorporated into our lives was less than self-evident. The immaculate surfaces of the line paintings early in the sixties could scarcely have predicted the protean radiance of a city wall—in no sense a painting—thirty years later in Pasadena: a field of change, not a field of monochrome. There was no shortcut to that embracing, within reason, of incident beyond control. In the interim there unfolded an unwavering if periodically halting inquiry into the way in which we are in the world.

If in the mid-fifties Irwin was, as he put it, a painter living "in the middle of nowhere," by 1957 there was the burgeoning Ferus Gallery on La Cienega Boulevard, spearheaded first by Edward Kienholz and Walter Hopps, then by Hopps and Irving Blum. And there were the young artists who gathered there—John Altoon, Billy Al Bengston, Craig Kauffman, Ed Moses among them—who introduced Irwin to Abstract Expressionism. Though Irwin was older than Bengston and Kauffman, it seemed to him that they knew more, and he promptly took a studio in the same building in order to learn what he needed to know.[6] The Abstract Expressionist paintings included in Irwin's 1959 exhibition at Ferus were imbued with what one critic described as "a flame-like turbulence . . . slashed in ridges and ribbons of pigment."[7] How, one might wonder, did Irwin get from there to the airport? It was a path staked out by questions. "My first real question concerned the arbitrariness of my paintings, the fact that six months after the 'emotion' of my involvement much of what I had done just seemed unnecessary."[8]

It was not the semblance of expressionist spontaneity but the "physics of perceptual structure" that Irwin found compelling in Willem de Kooning's paintings. "Perception is deeply tactile. The physicality of everything has a resonance. An area of orange has a particular denseness and weight, and how it occupies a space is as real as how you occupy that chair." The New York School artists, from Jackson Pollock to Barnett Newman, had formulated a visual vocabulary made of just such real forces.[9] There was hardly room for any vestige of the illusionistic nostalgia of figure and ground. Easier said than done, however, as the battles to wrestle figure and ground into one that were waged in the forties across de Kooning's paintings confirm. But the chasm to be crossed was clear enough to Newman, whose titles set the existentialist void against the phenomenological directive to be: *Euclidean Abyss* (1946–47) would be countered in the sixties by the declamatory present tense of *Be I* and *II* and the declarative immanence of *Here I, II,* and *III.*[10]

By the start of the 1970s Irwin had come to the conclusion that the issue at the core of the merging of figure and ground in painting is the collapsing of hierarchies of meaning, figure set off as meaningful against the meaningless ground. The continuum from foreground to background was a field in which systems of belief, power, and morality were exerted. What was important, who was powerful, were mapped in the ideal domain constructed by perspective—a system, as Heidegger saw it, in "complicity with a subject willed to mastery."[11] And so the journey from David's *The Coronation of Napoleon and Josephine* and Ingres's *Apotheosis of Homer* to Malevich's

Suprematist Composition: White on White and Mondrian's *Composition with Red, Yellow, and Blue* was charged with significance much beyond the pictorial. Painting was, for Irwin, a changing schema of consciousness.

But in 1959 Irwin had yet to think about any of this in quite these terms. He was in the studio twelve hours a day, seven days a week, trying to mold impetuous marks into plausible relationships, to transmute the arbitrary into the intended.

With the realization by the end of the 1950s that for him the rending of figure and ground could not continue, Irwin moved from the Abstract Expressionist paintings, which seemed "out-of-control," toward the resolute determination of a series of hand-held paintings, at their largest a foot square, enveloped by beautifully crafted wooden structures. But having banished large size and the gestural immediacy produced by felicitous "chance," what remained seemed limited and mannered, leading Irwin to confront what appeared to him to be his own superficiality. He stopped painting for the moment, until some months later, determined to do away with "Rorschachable" brushwork and marks that might be read as signs,[12] Irwin began to paint bars or lines across the once-again-large canvases of what he called "Pick-up Sticks" paintings.

Disciplined successors to the reckless strokes, the bars of color themselves enacted a drama of painterly structure, as they muscled one in front of another. But in time these too distilled themselves. Why, after all, did these elements angle in and out of space? In place of the profusion of color bars, four horizontal lines (1960-62), then three, and later, two horizontal lines (1963-64) took shape. The early lines

Untitled, ca. 1959-60
Oil on canvas in wood frame
20 3/4 x 21 inches
Collection of the artist

The Four Blues, 1961
Oil on canvas
65 5/8 x 65 1/8 inches
San Francisco Museum of Modern Art
Purchased with the aid of a gift of Rena Bransten

were "still composed, pictorial." But in the late lines, there was "no pictorial space in any overt way."[13] Identical at last in color in the late line paintings, line and field fended off unscathed monochrome only with tactile shifts. Palette-knifed lines were positioned on the brushed field, one line above and one below, "such that your eye could not really ever read the two lines simultaneously, nor even get involved with the kind of compositional thing." They read as "one line here, and one there;"[14] they read, that is, as if they were in our space. Disengaged from that "kind of compositional thing," the viewer was nudged into a new perceptual action.

If in the late lines Irwin had arrived at a scheme which for him defied any instantaneous unity of perception, then the larger import of this was a displacement: the central interaction took place not between compositional elements but between painting and viewer. Just as Ad Reinhardt's paintings were scarcely visible unless you spent time, and as Newman's paintings refused a grip on zip and field at once, so Irwin's paired lines deflected the viewer's gaze from line to field to line in a slowed, conscious process of perception.[15] For Newman, the force of time-made-palpable became clear not in the studio but confronting the Indian mounds in Ohio:

> There are no subjects—nothing that can be shown in a museum or even photographed; [it is] a work of art that cannot even be seen, so it is something that must be experienced there on the spot: The feeling [is] that here is the space; that these simple low mud walls make the space. . . . Suddenly one realizes that the sensation is not one of space or [of] an object in space. It has nothing to do with space and its manipulations. The sensation is the sensation of time. . . . Only time can be felt in private. Space is common property. . . . I insist on my experiences of sensations in time—not the *sense* of time but the physical *sensation* of time.[16]

The increasingly reductive abstraction of Irwin's paintings was rooted in his drive to work without allusion—to be more, not less, real. "I began to recognize the difference between imagery and physicality, that everything had both an imagery and a physicality." However nonobjective it might be, "imagery for me constituted representation, 're-presentation,' a second order of reality, whereas I was after a first order of presence. . . . The thing to realize is that the reduction was a reduction of imagery to get at physicality, a reduction of metaphor to get at presence."[17] Across an expanse of time made into felt duration, Irwin would sharpen our sense—better, our *sensation*—of being.

The stretchers of the earlier lines were crafted with unusual concern, and by 1963 the canvases were as taut as a drum, a responsive match for the strokes by which the artist applied the color. Irwin moved the 1/4-inch-thick strip frame behind, instead of beside, the painting. These concealed devices of transition quietly confirmed the inversion: the paintings were headed toward our world, not the one behind or across the wall. Irwin's monochrome canvases echo the "last paintings" announced by a succession of twentieth-century figures—early on Malevich and

Rodchenko, and later Reinhardt, who worked with lavish restraint within that domain he defined in terms of "what it is not"—"art is art-as-art and everything else is everything else"[18]—but for Irwin there were still five years of dots and discs to be painted, though he had glimpsed the terrain into which he would venture by the end of the decade.

The dot paintings of 1964-66 foretell Irwin's eventual move beyond the canvas, for in their fields of dots, alternately red and green until their density dissipates toward the edges, Irwin exactingly crafted the energy of a field of light across a subtly convex surface. The canvas literally swelled toward the viewer, six inches at its greatest depth in the center. In place of imagery, of gesture, of illusionistic space, Irwin had arrived at energies, as the red and green dots countered each other, neutralized as color, but reverberant, striking one critic as "a memory or 'after' image without the 'before.' "[19] Painting had here veered into the territory that interested Malevich when he declared that "solid matter does not exist in nature. There is only energy."[20]

In his elimination of the arbitrary, Irwin had initiated an unfolding investigation into the base structure of painting. That this could at the time have seemed somehow linked with the essentializing " 'Kantian' self-criticism" espoused by Clement Greenberg is suggested by Greenberg's proposal to include Irwin in the 1964 "Post Painterly Abstraction" exhibition at the Los Angeles County Museum of Art. It was, however naively, evident to Irwin that their intentions were at odds and he declined.[21] Greenberg's belief that "the arts, then, have been hunted back to their mediums, and there they have been isolated, concentrated and defined,"[22] suggested to Irwin a formalism oblivious to the content and context of the world, a protectionist enterprise that reduced circumstance to a nil that need not be acknowledged, that could barely be seen. The assumptions Irwin was challenging, however, were his own, much more than those of current critical discourse. Greenberg perhaps was looking for answers, for an end to the "confusion,"[23] Irwin, for questions, for a present, contingent condition.

Or, maybe Greenberg was locating a haven for painting within a culture of kitsch and co-opting commercialism.[24] But the sanctuary looked to Irwin like a defile. In 1965 Michael Fried's exhibition "Three American Painters: Kenneth Noland, Jules Olitski, Frank Stella" traveled from the Fogg Art Museum to the Pasadena Art Museum, overlapping in July with Maurice Tuchman's "New York School: The First Generation" at the Los Angeles County Museum of Art. Irwin was struck by the breadth of the compositions of Noland, Stella, Olitski, and Morris Louis (all included in "Post Painterly Abstraction"). Yet if no internal imperative, as Irwin saw it, precluded one more stripe, one more inch of painterly rivulet, then the expansiveness was curtailed nonetheless by the willful "delimitation" for which he finally could find no justification in his own painting. Irwin felt that, like him, they

Untitled, 1965-67
Sprayed acrylic lacquer
on shaped aluminum
60 inches diameter
Walker Art Center, Minneapolis
Purchased with a matching grant
from the Museum Purchase Plan,
the National Endowment for the
Arts and Art Center Acquisition
Fund, 1968

had "arrived at a point where they had a choice to make: whether to confine themselves to a frame, or break that. Was I going to follow my questions, or follow
current logic? The questions held water, so I went ahead."[25]

With the discs that followed the dots, made first of aluminum (ca. 1966-67) and
later of plastic (ca. 1967-69), Greenberg's postulate of edge ("the delimitation of flatness") and Fried's corollary of deductive structure (derived "from the literal character
of the picture-support")[26] would be turned inside out, as the paintings (as Irwin
viewed them), with their quatrefoil aureole of shadow, encircled—from within—the
continuum of light and its absence. From the center of the discs, modulated by nearly imperceptible gradations of color, to edge, to shadow, was an expanse of shifting
densities. "The here and there of the late lines is enfolded in an everywhere."[27] The
immaterial became palpable; physical substance turned ephemeral. Inescapably, the
visual field now extended from the painting to the space in which it was seen. Here
Irwin's thinking pursued that of Mondrian, who had suggested, to no avail, that
"the colors must be painted in the precise place where the work is to be seen," since
setting and light affect everything. In this theoretical break with the idea of the
timeless, immutable object, Mondrian had laid the grounds for a conditional art of
presence.[28]

Though by no means a Minimalist, Irwin had in the discs fulfilled all of the dread
conditions of the "literalist" (Minimal) art interrogated by Fried in the 1967 essay
"Art and Objecthood." The discs were endowed with presence rather than
autonomous presentness. Averting instantaneousness, they took time to see, sub-

merging themselves—however serenely—in the "hellish 'endlessness' " of object-hood. They were rampantly "theatrical" by Fried's definition—operating *between* the arts," in actual space and time—an "empty stage" unformed without the viewer's per-ceiving consciousness. But the discs—which were in no sense the objects of Fried's investigation and were most likely unknown to him at the time—were also less mate-rially substantial than the Judd boxes and Morris floor piece presented as evidence of the way in which "literalist work *depends* on the beholder, is *incomplete* without him."[29] And shortly there would be really no object made by Irwin even to cross-examine.

From epigraph to ending, Fried's essay fended off time and the body—mortality, really—in its language of instantaneity and pure opticality. In retrospect the allusion to Jonathan Edwards at the start suggests the Creation as a sort of theological analo-gy to instantaneity. Art here is revelatory and transcendent in opposition to this plodding, besieged existence. The schism between this view and Irwin's—which in 1967 would have appeared to be no more substantial than the shadows projected by the discs—really amounted to the divide between formalist self-referentiality with its absolutely internal completeness and an expanded field of shifting alliances and impure methods.

When Maurice Tuchman invited Irwin to participate in the Los Angeles County Museum's Art and Technology program in 1968, Irwin readily spotted the possibili-ties. While technology was not of particular interest, an opportunity to delve into ways of knowing, ways of thinking was. Having intuited a direction outside painting, the first issue was "Where am I? How do I think about space, how do I think about time?" How did scientists and mathematicians think about these questions, in an age of quarks, rubber sheet geometry, fractal space?[30]

Irwin spent three days with the physicist Richard Feynman, and soon was paired with Ed Wortz, head of the Life Sciences Department at Garrett Corporation. In order to understand how each thought, the two decided to create a succession of per-ceptual testing situations which would be experienced independently. After a day or so, they would meet to discuss what they had perceived, what each had found to be significant and how this was processed, what they might do with it. Irwin and Wortz believed the dialogue would benefit from the involvement of a third person. The artist James Turrell, who had studied psychology, joined them for several months. The various circumstances, which included time spent in an anechoic space and a Ganz field, were conceived to avoid preconceptions drawn from their backgrounds in science, psychology, and art. The collaboration proved decisive for Irwin and Wortz, changing the direction of both their lives.[31]

No plans were made to install anything in the museum. Irwin continued to work in a twenty-foot-square space which he had set up, while still working on the discs, in his Mildred Street studio in Venice. Here he experimented with projected and ambi-ent light, tautly stretched scrim, a rounding of the right angles of the room, shifts in the color of white from one wall to another. In the quiet of the studio, Irwin made the decisive transition from matter to energy as his means.[32]

The solitude of these studio investigations was happily disturbed when Wortz asked Irwin to help with the organization for NASA of the first National Symposium on Habitability. Irwin devised a succession of reworkings of a building which he secured to house the meetings at 72 Market Street in Venice. The space was transformed from a capsulelike enclosure, entered unceremoniously through a hole broken in the wall, on the first day; to a luminous, skylit openness, sheathed in front only by a translucent plane of nylon fabric on the second day; achieving finally a literal unboundedness as it opened onto the street, on the third day. That the panelists were influenced by the changing configurations of their environment was, surprisingly, unobserved by most, a follow-up questionnaire revealed.[33]

Focusing increasingly on perceptual processes, Irwin was intrigued by the nature of meditation and the emerging insights of electro-biofeedback. Two recently published, parallel studies, one of Japanese Zen Buddhist monks and one of masters and novices of raja-yoga in India, suggested that intention determined whether they habituated out or registered stimuli. Each study enlisted the same equipment to measure the physiological evidence of brain activity, heart rate, breathing, and so on, and focused on a group which meditated on nothingness. It was evident that whether they ignored pain or picked up the slightest sensation depended entirely on intention. The more practiced the mind, the more thorough the command.[34] This confirmed Irwin's mounting conviction, formed in the explorations with Wortz, that intention and reason (encompassing both logic and intuition) shape our experience.

As Irwin mulled over what to do about painting, which he was reluctant to relinquish, it seemed that perhaps it was a problem of dimension—two being less than three. A series of prismatic columns (1969-70) which lent material form to otherwise elusive light was one line of investigation. But Irwin was inclined to devise less physically discrete elements, as in the ongoing reworkings of the space on Mildred Street in 1968-69. Minimalism had done in sculpture, Irwin reasoned, what he had been doing in painting: moving toward a "here/there," dispensing with self-contained composition.[35] But the same problem persisted in three dimensions—the estrangement of objects from the enveloping fabric of experience. If painting no longer was viable for Irwin, then sculpture was no solution. It later appeared to Irwin that this had been predicted by Mondrian when he announced that *"the culture of particular form is approaching its end. The culture of determined relations has begun."*[36]

An invitation to create an installation in a small, somewhat quirky room at The Museum of Modern Art in New York proved an opportunity to make something of the thinking with which Irwin had been engrossed since embarking on the Art and Technology project. Here at MoMA in 1970 the work moved definitively beyond the environmental yearnings of the discs—their shadows played off and confounded the translucent object at their center—and of the columns—which fractured light into rays of color—and into the space itself. Irwin's MoMA work was strikingly insubstantial in its materials: a length of wire seven feet above the floor, about eighteen inches out from the wall, painted so that it emerged imperceptibly from the side walls and could not be fixed in space; a plane of scrim, dropped about four feet below the twelve-foot-high ceiling; alternately warm and cool white fluorescent tubes replacing those in the light fixtures. "The interaction of cool and warm fluorescents gave the effect of the light being fractured. When you fracture it, the light is activated—it becomes tactile, tangible. So it had the illusion of what a prism would do, but very subliminal."[37] None of this had any formal structure until stretched across the space itself. The conditional character of art, as of everything else, now had to be explicit, lest the forms made by the artist appear to have some life of their own.

Confronted with phenomena that could not be pinned down, that rebuffed any objectifying grip, the viewer was disarmed. The experience of the piece at MoMA could be described. Yet anything but the actual encounter was decidedly second-hand. Photographs, which Irwin long avoided, seemed as remote as a paraphrase of Gertrude Stein.

By the end of the sixties, Irwin had contemplated what people, literally suspended in space, cannot do without. Painting had been pushed toward a "limit of almost,"[38] though "almost" had proved not far enough. "You have to have a way of thinking equal to your questions." Irwin had some idea, by 1970, of what would have to go. His interest was in energy, not matter; process, not product; in the subject of art, not the objects through which we "illuminate what we have already come to know."[39]

This end, for Irwin, of painting was not without cost. It was lost not to its conventions, which could be defied, but to its inherent limitations: no matter how you shaped or expanded the edges, a painting intractably occupied a field less inclusive than do we. "I had lost my whole way of thinking."[40] In what sense might it have been his "whole way of thinking" when there was no image, nothing a word could pin down? How was he thinking? Abstractly? Concretely? Theoretically? "Painting had been both my process for selection and ordering of things and my philosophic method. . . ."[41] Was the work a phenomenological model, sliced from the world, at once real and a template?

In "dismantling" painting, Irwin had scrutinized its means and analyzed its motives. For it is motive that reveals where something is going: "something is whatever it is that makes its principal decisions."[42] Year after year Irwin had cast off what had become inessential: first the arbitrary; then marks that might be seen as signs; then interacting colors and forms that forced themselves one in front of another to wrest open pictorial space, or that settled into relationship with each other to become composition; later the mark itself; and finally the edge which defined a field

apart from the world. And here the discs had hit the wall, as it were. Painting, it seemed, when all was said and done, was a peripatetic, self-contained realm, carrying its own limits on its back.

Painting, that is, always played figure to the room's ground. Hierarchy persisted.[43] In his book *Being and Circumstance: Notes Toward a Conditional Art* (1985) Irwin would head up the essay's fourth section, focusing on the conditional, with an epigraph in which Mondrian looked ahead, "in a future perhaps remote, towards the end of *art as a thing separated from our surrounding environment*," to a time when art "will aid the creation of a surrounding not merely utilitarian or rational but also pure and complete in its beauty."[44] In 1970 Irwin had yet to read Mondrian's writings, but the next year he would be indelibly struck by the unfolding of Mondrian's thinking so lucidly revealed in the retrospective organized by the Guggenheim Museum in New York.[45] Perhaps Irwin sensed what Yve-Alain Bois would argue in 1986: that Mondrian's flattening of figure and ground was the threshold onto the non-fictive space of the viewer, that this was the abolition of hierarchical structure, tyrant of past thought and life. If art might for Mondrian operate as a "theoretical model"—"the plastic manifestation of a certain logic that he found at the root of all the phenomena of life"[46]—then for Irwin it would probe, from within experience, the workings of perception and reason, which for him were "at the base" of any understanding of "our existence in the world."[47]

The weight of the questions at which Irwin had arrived froze him for the moment, suspending any art-making. For the better part of a year, Irwin thought and looked, and made expeditions to the desert. For a while, desert sites of perceptible power were sometimes indicated with a stake. But the stake was a marker, pointing a vector of vision; it was nothing, in other words, in itself. And in any case, what he did during the years of the desert odyssey "was not art; it was to take time," to break from what he was doing, to work through these questions. "As long as you have something to do, you can't get to your questions."[48] From the lines wrought in the solitude of the Pier Avenue studio to the desert sightlines, Irwin had made his way toward Malevich's "desert of pure feeling." And Malevich's desert—"where nothing is real except feeling" and art is freed "from the ballast of objectivity"[49]—is "Husserl's phenomenal ground, a place where we may ask our one creative question: how might it be otherwise?"[50]

Away from the routine of the studio, there was a sort of four-a.m. clarity, undulled by the hum of normalcy. In the broad light of the desert it was evident that painting, and for that matter any self-contained objects, could scarcely be defended. Exhilarated by the magnitude of the "subject" of art, Irwin was confounded by the boundedness of the objects of art. The desert occasioned a disconcerting recognition: that he was no longer a studio artist, nor a gallery artist—how would he remain an art world artist? How would anyone know what he was doing?[51]

The end point of reduction, the sightlines were all attention. And intention. Irwin's desert pieces were willfully insubstantial, aggressively anti-formal: there was no form. This was not a tremendously effective strategy of communication. Nor was

Untitled, 1970
Cast acrylic column
Installation view
Northridge Shopping Center,
Northridge, California

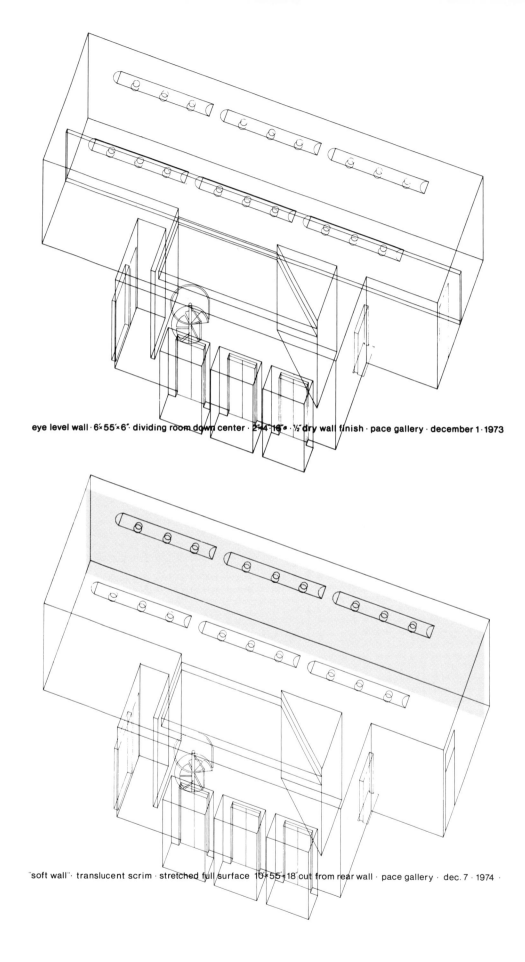

eye level wall · 6″×55′×6″ dividing room down center · 2″×4″-16″ o · ½″ dry wall finish · pace gallery · december 1 · 1973

"soft wall" · translucent scrim · stretched full surface 10′×55′×18″ out from rear wall · pace gallery · dec. 7 · 1974 ·

it meant to be, during this period of stocktaking and transition. The intention and attention played out in the sightlines belonged only to the artist: these could scarcely be expected to change the world.

Bereft of objects to be made, Irwin's days were increasingly weightless. It was sensible that Irwin decided to accept all invitations to speak and to create works—ideas developed in dialogue, work made "in response." His speaking invitations took him on a journey worthy of Kerouac. He would posit a question and try to answer it during a talk or residency, and then "wrastle with it" on the couple days drive to the next stop. An answer had, it seemed evident, the validity of its question.[52] As if to discern the limits of acting in response within an art-, not a desert-context, Irwin set to work with scrim, tape, string, and more scrim. Like answers, the pieces were conditional. During the seventies, circumstance landed Irwin most often in pristine white spaces. There were several things to recommend these venues: they were what was available; they were still in the art world; as Irwin worked his way from the point zero of the desert toward a way of again giving his ideas visibility and accessibility, they were foils of suitable simplicity.[53]

Eye Level Wall Division (1973) roughly bisected lengthwise the shoebox-like proportions of The Pace Gallery in New York, "doubling" the elongation of the room. While *Eye Level Wall Division* was thoroughly conceived in relation to site, it continued to function as something of an object. People peered over and examined it. The next year, *Soft Wall* (1974) stretched a plane of scrim floor to ceiling, eighteen inches in front of the expansive back wall at Pace. Floor, walls, and ceiling beyond the scrim were painted white, this volume reading as an opaque surface. *Eye Level Wall Division* was mysterious (why did he do it?), it could be scrutinized. *Soft Wall* was mystifying, undetectable. Unless the viewer spent time, the room seemed empty. *Soft Wall* opened onto the zone of the phenomenal, of "pure presence." "That is the door of perception, that's the door that gets you to the realm of determined relations." In its simplicity and confounding of perceptual complacency, *Soft Wall* struck Irwin as a statement of principle more than a piece of art.[54]

At this point Irwin began to read Hegel and Kant. His work had raised issues which people considered in philosophical terms; he wanted to participate in that discussion. Irwin found the processes of philosophic argument more compelling than any conclusions to which they might lead. While perception could be studied, the underlying nature of the transaction by which we are grounded in the world eluded explanation. In the writings of Edmund Husserl and Maurice Merleau-Ponty, Irwin found an articulation of four of his central convictions: 1. that perception is embodied, that we understand the world from within it; 2. that all experience is conditional, "that all understanding is understanding within a frame of reference," conceived in relation to the perceiver, grounded in circumstance;[55] 3. that intellectual habit and perceptual reflex obscure much of what we cannot deal with quantitatively and objectively; and 4. that we can cut through our instrumentalized vision only by setting aside our assumptions, a process Husserl laid out in his discussion of a phenomenological reduction and its technique of "bracketing."

Eye Level Wall Division, 1973
Soft Wall, 1974
The Pace Gallery, New York

From 1975 through 1977 Irwin's "Continuing Responses" at the Fort Worth Art Museum operated as a series of experimental strategies for impelling attention. Lines of string, planes of paint and scrim were installed in stairwells, offices, hallways, now and then in a gallery. Richard Koshalek, Fort Worth's director at the time, encouraged Irwin's research approach: there was no pressure for a product. All of the responses were derived from and aimed toward a perceptual realm which Irwin would formulate in opposition to the domain of cognition: "direct experience (responsibility) vs. prestructured expectation, phenomena vs. permanence, presence vs. abstraction. . . ."[56] Twelve "incidental sculptures" drew the observer out into Fort Worth itself in pursuit of found phenomena intended anew by the artist. It was at Fort Worth that Irwin came to grips with his ambitions for "the end of *art as a thing separated from our surrounding environment*," as Mondrian had put it, an end that is "at the same time a new beginning."[57]

In 1977 Irwin was ready to theorize the import of the objectless space into which he had moved. His exhibition that spring at the Whitney Museum of American Art in New York read as a schema that projected its own implications. Emerging from the

String Line — Light Volume, 1975
From the series
"Continuing Responses"
Black string
96 x 120 x 360 inches
The Modern Art Museum
of Fort Worth
Museum purchase:
The Benjamin J. Tillar
Memorial Trust

Yard

elevator onto the fourth floor, the museum goer entered a large, puzzling space, luminous, charged with energy, empty of objects. The natural light was sharpened and made palpable by the scrim which hovered at a perceptually unfixable distance within the 120-foot-long gallery. Since all artificial light had been eliminated, the brightness diminished dramatically from the window at the left toward the far end of the scrim at the right. The wall opposite the window, which normally reflects the brightness of the window's light, was painted the gray to which the illumination of scrim and walls had dimmed. The geometry of the space snapped into focus.[58] A black line ran along the bottom of the scrim, at eye level, and continued around the four walls of the room, which became a diagram of itself: from ceiling grid through black linear rectangle, to the black plane of the floor. Even as it elucidated the space, the black line baffled the viewer's efforts to locate the scrim division with any precision.

The Whitney's fourth floor, as Irwin had approached it, contained five essential conditions. 1. The interior space is vast by the standards of New York City. 2. The window is a dominant element. Given its angle of foreshortening, it constructs a "classic pictorial situation," overwhelming in its powerful scale and real world content. 3. The gallery is entered midway between the wall containing the window and the one across from it. 4. The black plane of the slate floor establishes a real sense of

New York Projection:
Line Rectangle —
World Trade Center, 1977
Installed during "Robert Irwin"
(April 16-May 29, 1977) at
Whitney Museum of
American Art, New York

place. 5. The beehive grid ceiling (bared of light fixtures for the exhibition) "is a geometry that diminishes into pattern."[59] These circumstances, usually taken for granted, were intensified and rendered alternately ineffable and inexplicably clear in a strategy devised to suspend the "natural standpoint."[60]

Two *New York Projections* moved beyond the frame of the museum altogether, refiguring the works that Irwin had devised there. The floor plane of the Whitney was recast as a freshly painted black square plane inscribed in the intersection of 42nd Street and Fifth Avenue. The linear black rectangle of the fourth floor was reworked in a *Line Rectangle* of rope outlining the astonishing volume between the World Trade Center towers. The ceiling grid was to have been echoed in a *Projection* which went unrealized: a grid delineated by a laser and mirrors at about the fourth floor level of the buildings flanking four blocks of Park Avenue.[61] Extending the extrapolations from the museum space, the catalogue included aerial photographs of the city: a composition of shadow planes cast in the raking afternoon sun by the buildings along Park Avenue; a succession of grids of New York streets and buildings; and the rectangular plane of Central Park outlined at night by mercury vapor light. These photographs, which Irwin purchased, were not intended as an art form, but rather pressed the question posed by the exhibition as a whole: "if we take words like perception, aesthetics, creativity as bearing directly on art, can we hold the dialogue for art to be the equal of making?" The answer, for Irwin, was no. In its progressive foray into a zone beyond made objects, the Whitney project evinced "the pure void of concept." "Art is a non-thing. That is, it has no actual physical properties, or, if you wish, it has infinite physical properties. It is whatever we posit it to be."[62]

"Notes Toward a Model," the essay which Irwin wrote for the catalogue, conceived the "infinite subject" of art to be aesthetic perception[63]—by which Irwin meant, no doubt, a perception that acknowledges the gradations of light across the room, and observes the fluctuating shadow simulacra of the city's architecture, rather than simply finding the door. "By these words, the 'primacy of perception,' " wrote Merleau-Ponty, "we mean that the experience of perception is our presence at the moment when things, truths, values are constituted for us; that perception is a nascent *logos*. . . . It is not a question of reducing human knowledge to sensation, but of assisting at the birth of this knowledge. . . ."[64]

Exhibition and catalogue together probed the transitions by which our "conceptual structures become . . . hidden orthodoxies," a process that starts fresh with perception and ends entrenched with formalism. From straight line, to Euclidean geometry, to grid, to city; from frame and plane to "flatness and the delimitation of flatness,"[65] we operate within useful "compounded abstractions."[66] But all of these beautifully

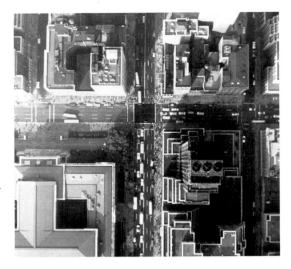

New York Projection:
**Black Plane — Fifth Avenue
and 42nd Street,** 1977
Installed during "Robert Irwin"
(April 16-May 29, 1977) at
Whitney Museum of
American Art, New York

compounded structures come, finally, from "the
primitive world of the senses, of perception."
Hence the riveting centrality of *Scrim Veil—Black
Rectangle—Natural Light* in the museum. Everything
beyond this world of perception is by degrees
abstract. But both sensate experience and compounded structures are true: "how we come to hold our
truths—this, then, is the point of the model. . . ."[67]

If the Whitney project inquired into "what we
can know," then there was also the question of how
these projections and this model were to work in the world. Even a critic who
admired the rope outline of the volume between the two tallest buildings in the
world found the black plane intersection invisible unless "from the vantage point of
hands and knees."[68] With no object and no art space, what would the extended
frame of reference be? If art has no absolute form nor timeless agenda, defined
instead by tacit agreement among those involved at any given time,[69] with whom
was this agreement, out on Fifth Avenue at 42nd Street?

It was as if the urban rhythms of Mondrian's *Broadway Boogie-Woogie* and the austere planes of Malevich's *Suprematist Composition: White on White* had returned to the
world from which they had been deduced. Irwin's moves are slighter by far than their
effects, always at least one dimension shy of what they bring into play. This is not
reticence. Art is here a schema embedded in the world. It is a Trojan horse passing
as a darting line of light in the airport. Otherwise it would be life, or architecture.
Otherwise, it wouldn't be a bracket, a desert of pure feeling. There would only be
another place.

Perception is for Irwin formed by mind and body, fueled by reason and feeling,
grounded in circumstance; what we see is always partial, individual. "I will never
know how you see red, and you will never know how I see it," Merleau-Ponty con-
cluded.[70] "How we perceive," Irwin has reflected, "is at the base of how we reason
our existence in the world from a particular perspective. And how we reason is at the
base of how we perceive." If we think quantitatively rather than qualitatively—
inquiring of an abstract painting "what is it?"—then too we have instrumentalized our
way of being in the world.[71] "It is because we are through and through compounded
of relationships with the world that for us the only way to become aware of the fact
is to suspend the resultant activity, to refuse it our complicity," Merleau-Ponty wrote,
"or yet again, to put it 'out of play'. . . . The best formulation of the reduction is probably that given by Eugen Fink, Husserl's assistant, when he spoke of 'wonder' in the
face of the world."[72] What begins in perception returns, finally, to affect the world.
"Tacitly, by implication," as we dwell within a shifted world view, we reshape,
"covertly" perhaps, the structures of society, the fabric of thought.[73]

Portal Park Slice, 1980
John W. Carpenter Park, Dallas
Aerial view, detail

In the years that separated the shadow grid along Park Avenue from the
scrim shadow planes which hover like perceptual propositions in the atrium
of the Old Post Office building in Washington, D.C., Irwin pursued the
cues of the *New York Projections*. From the late seventies, Irwin has moved
increasingly into the domain of outdoor, sometimes civic, space. A sleek
700-foot-long Cor-Ten plane intercepted and counterbalanced a complex
tangle of expressways, streets, and park space into Dallas's *Portal Park Slice*.
Violet-blue planes of vinyl-coated chainlink mesh were interposed like an
axonometric drawing across a stand of eucalyptus trees at the University of
California, San Diego. Violet flowers blossom below, as if "stained" in some fantasy
of Mondrian, the grove taking on the aura of a jacaranda tree. In Pasadena, a small
city square, designed for sitting, opens onto a cobalt-violet wall. Across this back-
drop, the light will fluctuate, as if this were a flattened incarnation of a scenario
called up in *Being and Circumstance*: "Picture a wall before you. This wall is curved,
rough, and red. A cloud passes before the sun and the wall becomes flat, smooth,
and violet. Now I can walk along the wall and reaffirm its being curved, and I can
run my hands over its surface to reaffirm its roughness. But what am I to do about
the violet? Is the violet not real? And what happens to my sense of reality when the
wall just as suddenly turns back to being red, or is influenced into becoming some
other color?"[74] These works might at first look schematic, but they confound the
promise of clarity. The eye cannot fix the shadow planes, or the lambent light
amidst breeze-driven leaves, cannot pin it all down at once. Cognition relinquishes
its hold; attention builds momentum. The gaze is deflected back onto the surround
of light, space, trees, architecture, time.[75]

Two Running Violet V Forms, 1983
Stuart Collection
University of California,
San Diego

If "non-objective" had in 1977 meant "non-object" to Irwin, then that had been a step en route to the realm of "determined relations." And anything, it had turned out, even objects, could be enlisted "in relation."[76] The works since the Whitney seem wildly disparate, as if Irwin were a dozen artists. If you look, that is, at what he made. But Irwin has long since positioned himself at the conditional end of a continuum he outlined in *Being and Circumstance*, which runs from site-dominant, site-adjusted, and site-specific, to site-conditioned/determined. At this far end of openness, each situation is approached without preconception, each circumstance particular, unforeseen: "since a conditional art, by its own definition, possesses no transcendent criteria (truths), it can have no grounds for predetermining (preplanning) its actions."[77]

By 1977 there was no object of Irwin's making. Fifteen years later there are places, paths, planes of lawn, lines of light: *"landscape* and *not-landscape,"* as Rosalind Krauss figured it in "Sculpture in the Expanded Field," *"architecture* plus *not- architecture."*[78] For the work is thought, materialized in one form or another depending on the situation. "Revolution doesn't cause change; change causes revolution," Irwin would add to his belief that "ideas are of no value if they don't change your life."[79] In art, as in philosophy, we are without other motives: here then is the point of the "pure void of concept," the "infinite subject." This is how the qualitative outstrips the quantitative. In public space and private time, Irwin's works are limpid zones of being, enfolding spheres of circumstance. At the Whitney, in the eucalyptus grove, in the afternoon in Pasadena, "you just have to experience it," "here," now.

Notes

Interviews are with the author, in San Diego, except as otherwise noted.

1. Interview with Robert Irwin, Summer 1992. *Sound Chasing Light* was proposed by Irwin in 1982.

2. Tony Smith's account is quoted in Michael Fried, "Art and Objecthood," *Artforum* 5, no. 10 (June 1967): 19, and retold in Hal Foster, "The Crux of Minimalism," in Howard Singerman, ed., *Individuals: A Selected History of Contemporary Art 1945-1986* (Los Angeles: The Museum of Contemporary Art, 1986), p.173.

3. *Smoke* was made in plywood for the 1967 exhibition "Scale as Content: Ronald Bladen, Barnett Newman, Tony Smith." See Andrew Hudson, "Scale as Content: Bladen, Newman, Smith at the Corcoran," *Artforum* 6, no. 4 (December 1967): 45-47.

4. See Foster, "The Crux of Minimalism," p.173, and Fried, "Art and Objecthood," p.19. The phrase is Rosalind Krauss's ("Sculpture in the Expanded Field," *October*, no. 8 (Spring 1979), reprinted in Rosalind E. Krauss, *The Originality of the Avant-Garde and Other Modernist Myths* (Cambridge, Mass.: MIT Press, 1985)). In Krauss's crucial essay, Irwin figures as one of "the first artists to explore the possibilities of architecture plus not-architecture." (*The Originality of the Avant-Garde*, p.287.)

5. See Joan Didion, *Slouching Towards Bethlehem* (New York: Farrar, Straus and Giroux, 1968).

6. Robert Irwin, "Notes Toward a Model," *Robert Irwin* (New York: Whitney Museum of American Art, 1977), p.23; Lawrence Weschler, *Seeing is Forgetting the Name of the Thing One Sees: A Life of Contemporary Artist Robert Irwin* (Berkeley and Los Angeles: University of California Press, 1982), pp.47-49; Calvin Tomkins, "Profiles: A Touch for the Now—Walter Hopps," *The New Yorker*, 29 July 1991, 42; interview with Irwin, Summer 1992.

7. Jules Langsner, "Cremean, Gottlieb, Irwin," *Art News* 58, no. 4 (Summer 1959): 60.

8. Robert Irwin, "Notes Toward a Model," p.23. Irwin had thought about this five years earlier in "The State of the Real: Robert Irwin Discusses the Activities of an Extended Consciousness—Part 1," compiled by Jan Butterfield, *Arts Magazine* 46, no. 8 (Summer 1972): 49. See Weschler, p.155.

9. Interviews with Robert Irwin, Summer 1992, Fall 1991, Spring 1992. See Weschler, pp.55-57.

10. See Sally Yard, "The Angel and the *demoiselle*: Willem de Kooning's *Black Friday*," *Record of the Art Museum, Princeton University* 50, no. 2 (1991): 2-25. For eloquent and pertinent considerations of these and other works by Newman, see Jean-Francois Lyotard, "Newman: The Instant," *The Lyotard Reader*, ed. Andrew Benjamin (Cambridge, Mass.: Basil Blackwell, 1989), esp. pp.248-49; and Yve-Alain Bois, "Perceiving Newman" (1988) *Painting as Model* (Cambridge, Mass.: MIT Press, 1990), pp.187-213, esp. pp.201-203.

11. Hal Foster, preface to Hal Foster, ed., *Vision and Visuality* (Seattle: Bay Press, 1988), Dia Art Foundation, Discussions in Contemporary Culture, no. 2, p.xiv. Irwin's consideration of figure/ground can be followed in "The State of the Real," pp.48-49, "Notes Toward a Model," p.31; Robert Irwin, *Being and Circumstance: Notes Toward a Conditional Art* (Larkspur Landing, Calif.: Lapis Press, 1985), pp.15, 18; and Robert Irwin, "The Hidden Structures of Art" (1992), p.22; and was discussed in interviews of Fall 1991.

12. Interview with Irwin, Summer 1992. See Weschler, pp.61-62 for a discussion of this moment.

13. Interview with Irwin, Summer 1992.

14. Irwin quoted in Weschler, p.75; interview with Irwin, Summer 1992. Irwin arrived at the dimensions after lengthy deliberation. The sometimes nearly square, other times actually seven-foot-square line paintings were followed by the 82 1/2 x 84 1/2 inch dot paintings. See Weschler, p.89.

15. See Yve-Alain Bois, "The Limit of Almost," in *Ad Reinhardt* (New York: The Museum of Modern Art, and Los Angeles: The Museum of Contemporary Art, 1991), p.28 for a consideration of Ad Reinhardt's "narrativization" of the viewer's gaze. See also Bois, "Perceiving Newman," p.203.

16. Barnett Newman, "Ohio, 1949," *Barnett Newman—Selected Writings and Interviews*, ed. John P. O'Neill (New York: Knopf, 1990), pp. 174-75.

17. Irwin quoted in Weschler, pp.61, 200; see Irwin, "The State of the Real," p.49.

18. Ad Reinhardt, "Art-As-Art," in *Ad Reinhardt* (New York: The Museum of Modern Art, and Los

Two Running Violet V Forms,
1983
Stuart Collection
University of California,
San Diego

Angeles: The Museum of Contemporary Art, 1991), p.121.

19. Diane Waldman, "Reviews and Previews: Robert Irwin," *Art News* 65, no. 9 (January 1967):14.

14. See Philip Leider's remarkable discussion of the paintings in *Robert Irwin, Kenneth Price* (Los Angeles: Los Angeles County Museum of Art, 1966), unnumbered pages. See Irwin, "The State of the Real," p.49.

20. Kazimir Malevich, "Futurism-Suprematism" (1921) in *Kazimir Malevich* (Los Angeles: Armand Hammer Museum of Art and Cultural Center, 1990), p.178.

21. Interview with Irwin, Fall 1991. See Weschler, p.79. Greenberg discussed " 'Kantian' self-criticism" in "Modernist Painting," *Art and Literature*, no. 4 (Spring 1965): 193.

22. Clement Greenberg, "Towards a Newer Laocoon" (1940), in *Clement Greenberg: The Collected Essays and Criticism* vol. 1, "Perceptions and Judgments, 1939-1944," ed. John O'Brian (Chicago: University of Chicago Press, 1986), p.32. Irwin would observe: "For us to see 'art' as a confined pictorial world is a very *learned* logic. For example, it takes the same kind of logical distortion to see a canvas as flat, as was being proposed, as it took to see it as a window, when in fact it is neither. It is a three-dimensional form protruding from the wall." Quoted in Ira Licht, *Robert Irwin* (Chicago: The Museum of Contemporary Art, 1975), p.4.

23. Greenberg, "Towards a Newer Laocoon," p.24.

24. See Clement Greenberg, "Avant-Garde and Kitsch" (1939), *Art and Culture* (Boston: Beacon, 1961), esp. pp.8-9. See also Greenberg, "Towards a Newer Laocoon," p.32: "The arts lie safe now, each within its 'legitimate' boundaries. . . ."

25. Interview with Irwin, Summer 1992.

26. It was in "After Abstract Expressionism" (*Art International* 6, no. 8 (October 25, 1962): 30) that Greenberg declared: "By now it has been established, it would seem, that the irreducible essence of pictorial art consists in but two constitutive conventions or norms: flatness and the delimitation of flatness; and that the observance of merely these two norms is enough to create an object which can be experienced as a picture: thus a stretched or tacked-up canvas already exists as a picture—though not necessarily as a *successful*

one." See Greenberg, " 'American-Type' Painting" (1955, 1958), in *Art and Culture*, pp.226-27 for a consideration of "edge." See Michael Fried, *Three American Painters: Kenneth Noland, Jules Olitski, Frank Stella* (Cambridge, Mass.: Fogg Art Museum, 1965), pp.40-41.

27. Interview with Irwin, Summer 1992.

28. Piet Mondrian, "The New Plastic in Painting" (1917), in *The New Art—The New Life: The Collected Writings of Piet Mondrian*, ed. and trans. by Harry Holtzman and Martin S. James (Boston: G. K. Hall, 1986), p.37. See Yve-Alain Bois's "New York City" (*Critical Inquiry* 14, no. 2 (Winter 1988): 268) which drew my attention to this striking passage. Interview with Irwin, Summer 1992. See Ronald J. Onorato's "Being There: Context, Perception, and Art in the Conditional Tense," in *Individuals* for an illuminating discussion of recent art conceived in relation to context.

29. See Fried, "Art and Objecthood," esp. pp.21-22. While "endlessness" belongs to Fried's argument (p.22), its "hellish" qualifier is Hal Foster's ("The Crux of Minimalism," p.174). "Empty stage" is Leider's phrase (unnumbered pages), enlisted in describing the dot paintings. I am indebted to Foster's reading of "Art and Objecthood" as an argument at once judicial and theological. Fried pins down an understanding of presence ("Art and Objecthood," p.16): "Furthermore, the presence of literalist art, which Greenberg was the first to analyze, is basically a theatrical effect or quality—a kind of *stage* presence. It is a function, not just of the obtrusiveness and, often, even aggressiveness of literalist work, but of the special complicity which that work extorts from the beholder. Something is said to have presence when it demands that the beholder take it into account, that he take it *seriously*—and when the fulfillment of that demand consists simply in being *aware* of it and, so to speak, in acting accordingly."

30. Interview with Irwin, Summer 1992.

31. Ibid.; see also the account in Jane Livingston and Maurice Tuchman, *A Report on the Art and Technology Program of the Los Angeles County Museum of Art: 1967-1971* (Los Angeles: Los Angeles County Museum of Art, 1971), pp.127-43; and Weschler, p.131.

32. Weschler, pp.112, 124; Edward Levine, "Robert Irwin: World Without Frame," *Arts*

Magazine 50, no. 6 (February 1976): 76; interview with Irwin, Summer 1992.

33. Interview with Irwin, Summer 1992. See Weschler, pp.131-33 for an account that draws on Wortz's recollections; and Livingston and Tuchman, pp.140-43.

34. Interview with Irwin, Fall 1991.

35. Interview with Irwin, Summer 1992.

36. Piet Mondrian, "Plastic Art and Pure Plastic Art" (1936), in *The New Art—The New Life: The Collected Writings of Piet Mondrian*, p.293.

37. Interview with Irwin, Summer 1992.

38. See Bois on Reinhardt, "The Limit of Almost."

39. Interviews with Irwin, Fall 1991, Spring 1992. See Weschler, pp.111, 124.

40. Interview with Irwin, Fall 1991.

41. Irwin, *Being and Circumstance*, p.12. See also Weschler, pp.159-60.

42. Irwin, "Notes Toward a Model," p.23; interview with Irwin, Spring 1992.

43. See Levine, "Robert Irwin: World without Frame," p.75. See also Weschler, pp.108-109.

44. Piet Mondrian, "Plastic Art and Pure Plastic Art," pp.299-300.

45. Interview with Irwin, Spring 1991.

46. Yve-Alain Bois, "Painting: The Task of Mourning" (1986), *Painting as Model*, p.240.

47. Interview with Irwin, Spring 1992.

48. Interview with Irwin, Summer 1992. See also Weschler, p.161; Licht, p.12.

49. Kazimir Malevich, "Suprematism" (1927), in Robert L. Herbert, ed., *Modern Artists on Art* (Englewood Cliffs, N.J.: Prentice-Hall, 1964), pp.94-95. See Irwin, *Being and Circumstance*, p.24.

50. Interview with Irwin, Fall 1991; Irwin, "The Hidden Structures of Art," pp.30, 18. See Irwin, *Being and Circumstance*, p.14.

51. Interview with Irwin, Summer 1992.

52. Irwin recounts the decision to work "in response" in "Notes Toward a Model," p.23; interview with Irwin, Summer 1992. See Weschler, pp.163-65; and "Robert Irwin: On the Periphery of Knowing," interview by Jan Butterfield (*Arts Magazine* 50, no. 6 (February 1976): 74) for accounts of this period.

53. Interview with Irwin, Summer 1992. See Weschler, p.182.

54. Interviews with Irwin, Summer 1992, Spring 1992.

55. Interview with Irwin, Summer 1992.

56. Irwin, *Being and Circumstance*, p.89.

57. Mondrian, "Plastic Art and Pure Plastic Art," p.299.

58. Roberta Smith's incisive writing on Irwin's 1975 installation at the Museum of Contemporary Art in Chicago suggested the apt word "snap." ("Robert Irwin: The Subject is Sight," *Art in America* 64, no. 2 (March-April 1976): 69.)

59. Interview with Irwin, Summer 1992.

60. These are Edmund Husserl's words. (*Ideas*, trans. W. R. Boyce Gibson (New York: Collier, 1962), pp.96, 103).

61. Interview with Irwin, Spring 1992.

62. Interview with Irwin, Summer 1992. See Irwin, "The Hidden Structures of Art," p.32.

63. Irwin, "Notes Toward a Model," p.31.

64. Maurice Merleau-Ponty, *The Primacy of Perception*, ed. James M. Edie (Evanston, Ill.: Northwestern University Press, 1964), p.25.

65. See note 26.

66. Irwin, "Notes Toward a Model," pp.24-25.

67. Interview with Irwin, Summer 1992; Irwin, "Notes Toward a Model," p.29.

68. Interview with Irwin, Summer 1992. Hayden Herrera, "Manhattan Seven," *Art in America* 65, no. 4 (July-August 1977): 52-53.

69. Interview with Irwin, Spring 1992.

70. Merleau-Ponty, *Primacy*, p.17.

71. Interview with Irwin, Spring 1992.

72. Maurice Merleau-Ponty, *Phenomenology of Perception*, trans. Colin Smith (London: Routledge, 1962), p.xiii.

73. Interview with Irwin, Fall 1991; Irwin, "The Hidden Structures of Art," pp.39, 40.

74. Irwin, *Being and Circumstance*, pp.21-22.

75. See Irwin's discussion of 48 *Shadow Planes* in *Being and Circumstance*, p.107.

76. Interview with Irwin, Summer 1992.

77. Irwin, *Being and Circumstance*, p.23.

78. Krauss, "Sculpture in the Expanded Field," *The Originality of the Avant-Garde and Other Modernist Myths*, p.287.

79. Interview with Irwin, Spring 1992; see Weschler, pp.201, 178, 169.

The Lucky U, 1959
Oil on canvas
71 x 84 inches
Estate of Helen Jacobs

Hands-on: Irwin and Abstract Expressionism

John Hallmark Neff

For twenty years I'd thought in terms of making objects; I'd worked out my ideas by working on physical things.[1]

Robert Irwin with
self-portrait, ca. 1951

When Robert Irwin sold his studio and its contents in 1970, he'd been painting for over half his life. By then the issue was clear: to pursue his study of perceptual phenomena outdoors as single-mindedly as he'd engaged painting indoors, he could no longer tie himself to discrete objects and their making. So painting—and his studio—had to go.

Along the way, painting, in the intellectual as well as the physical sense, had become Irwin's most important tool to clarify and to focus his intentions. Painting was his way of thinking, of asking questions and making decisions: paintings were the result.

To physically make each painting, to ponder each assumption, decision, and mark, was the price of admission to the ideas that intrigued Irwin most. Even later on, when he could intuit where an idea might take him (as began to happen with his late line and dot paintings) he would not shortcut the trial and error testing of his hunches. To do otherwise was to forgo information, the insights and unexpected events that occurred when he worked hands-on. It was as a painter, through an extraordinarily close reading of his own diverse "paintings" and their effects, that he first pursued his growing obsession with perceptual processes—that "attending to" of the "incidental" phenomena of everyday experience that remains today the focus of his activity.

Painting then was many things to Irwin (it was, for example, a relatively cheap way to conduct perceptual research), but most of all painting became an interrogatory process that edged him toward one decision—and one painting—at a time.

This notion of Robert Irwin *painter* may surprise those aware only of the later installations, his often ephemeral interventions with scrim or light. But although Irwin has not made an easel painting for twenty-five years, painting continues to inform his thinking (and so his practice) in fundamental as well as subtle ways.

He has remarked that "I didn't begin to ask [myself] interesting questions" until the late line paintings of 1962-64, in which he asked himself how to not make a painting. Irwin realizes now, however, that it was earlier, during his stint as an "Abstract Expressionistophile"—learning from his younger peers around the Ferus Gallery—that he first became aware that there were questions to ask.[2]

Abstract Expressionism is neither as monolithic nor as focused as it was once assumed to be. Recent studies of this diversity—West Coast, East Coast, European, and Japanese, large and small scale,[3] gestural and field, and first, second, and even third generation—permit us to view Irwin's practice of Abstract Expressionism for what it offered at the time to young artists everywhere: a liberation from local orthodoxies and moribund styles, and a loose methodology and practice that allowed a great many individualists to find themselves artistically. As a rite of passage it cannot be underestimated, though just the opposite is true for its available means of transmission and the question of influence. Without denying the appeal of Willem de Kooning and Franz Kline in particular for Irwin and his contemporaries in Los Angeles in the mid and late 1950s, it is clear that for many of the artists in the group with whom Irwin worked most closely, the work and example of artists teaching or working in San Francisco had the most immediate impact, Clyfford Still, Hassel Smith, and Frank Lobdell foremost among them. Still was revered for his no-nonsense approach to painting, for "just putting it down." Philip Guston, too, who'd grown up in Los Angeles and was suspect in New York for his alleged "French" facture was appreciated in Los Angeles for precisely that: his sensuous painting surfaces and lighter, subtle color. Still and Guston define the parameters of Irwin's work of 1958-62, but so, too, do unexpected artists such as Giorgio Morandi and Joan Mitchell, and later, the ideas if not practice of Ad Reinhardt.

Seldom exhibited, uneven, poorly documented, Irwin's Abstract Expressionist paintings from 1958-61 were the first works of his artistic maturity. The survivors comprise three distinct groups, each group further differentiated into earlier and later variations. These are: 1) the large Sawtelle paintings of 1958-59, including the later so-called "Zen-titled" or Zen paintings; 2) the small hand-held paintings (and a group of oil on paper paintings) from 1959-60; and 3) the few but critical Pick-up Sticks paintings made in Ocean Park during 1960-61, which quickly led Irwin into the early line paintings.

Irwin, ca. 1951

For Irwin, born in 1928 in Long Beach, California and coming of age in 1940s Los Angeles, wanting to be an artist without really knowing why, painting was the

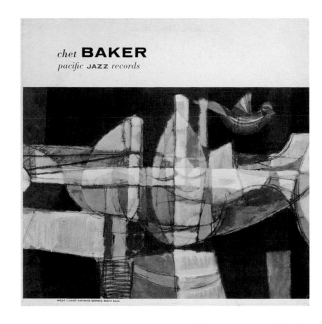

chet **BAKER**
pacific JAZZ *records*

WEST COAST ARTISTS SERIES: Robert Irwin

Chet Baker album cover
Pacific Jazz Records
Cover painting by
Robert Irwin
Cover design by
William Claxton

obvious option. As a gifted if unsophisticated painter, he steadily achieved a regional reputation in juried shows during the Truman and Eisenhower years, first locally, then in San Francisco, then nationally—what he calls his "talent awards." Recognition came early—even for an album cover commissioned in 1955 to align younger L.A. artists with the West Coast jazz scene.[4]

Irwin considers none of this of any consequence, the product of a facile hand ("magic wrists") and a natural ability to draw and paint that was in fact an obstacle to his learning more. This hit Irwin hard in 1957 at the opening of his first solo gallery exhibition at the prestigious Felix Landau Gallery on North La Cienega Boulevard's gallery row. Seeing his large abstractions clearly for the first time—large contrasting shapes horizontally disposed, suggesting landscape, drawn more than painted in the current "fractured Modern" style—he was appalled.

Resolved to pursue painting seriously and already "behind" after two stints in the Army and an indifferent education, he realized at twenty-eight that he had no choice but "to jettison [his] talent and start over again—from scratch."[5]

In the aftermath of the Landau show he'd realized that he had much to learn from a group of younger painters up the street at the newly opened Ferus Gallery, and he "just started to be around." Ferus Gallery is a subject unto itself, but suffice it to say that Irwin's reception was not overwhelming.[6] Walter Hopps, with Ed Kienholz one of the co-founders, recalls that other painters "kind of put up their noses," but Irwin tolerated it, very much the student of Craig Kauffman (b. 1932), Billy Al Bengston (b. 1934) and Ed Moses (b. 1926). The natural leader of the gang was John Altoon (1925–1969), whom Irwin had followed behind at Dorsey High as "art superstars" numbers one and two respectively. It was Bengston, who'd been making Abstract Expressionist ceramics[7] and was unabashedly enthusiastic about San Francisco-style Abstract Expressionism, who brought Irwin into the studio on Santa Monica Boulevard and introduced him to the cheap oil-based Bay Paint they were using ("half-way to housepaint"). Irwin recalls making some "experimental A-E works" as well as some "wash paintings," half stain, half textured, that he subsequently destroyed.

In the spring of 1958, Irwin moved further west to an old one-story frame building divided into two storefronts on Sawtelle Boulevard. Ed Moses was next door, behind a distribution shop for traveling salesmen. Irwin remembers taking the front space, sharing it later with Craig Kauffman. Allen Lynch, another painter, took the smaller space in back. It was a fluid situation. Artists came and went. They talked (though it was mostly a non-verbal association), argued, fought, horsed around, and hung out at the tough bar around the corner on Santa Monica, The Lucky U. (Altoon, Irwin, and others would name paintings after it). Toward the end of 1958 Irwin was invited to join

Untitled, ca. 1959-60
Oil on canvas in wood frame
11 1/4 x 11 1/2 inches
Collection of the artist

the "New Ferus" which reorganized and moved across La Cienega, one of seven Los Angeles artists joining an equal number from San Francisco. To prepare himself for his first show there, Irwin "went through a tremendous act of will. . . . He read everything in English he could get his hands on about Zen. . . . Beckett. Bob was really into it."[8]

In an unusual departure for Ferus, Irwin's exhibition in March, 1959, was accompanied by a small catalogue with four black-and-white halftone reproductions, a checklist, and, inside the front cover, eight lines of Cold Mountain poetry.[9] Twelve paintings and a group of "collage studies" were listed; it is probable that only eight or nine were shown. One review appeared in *Art News;* a painting or two sold; some he destroyed. One of the best, *The Lucky U,* was later juried into the 1959 Los Angeles County Museum Annual Exhibition of Artists of Los Angeles and Vicinity.

Although referred to as his Zen paintings, the catalogue suggests that the work broke down into two groups, a group of slightly smaller "Sawtelle" paintings from 1958 that were apparently lighter in color and more gestural than the early 1959 group of darker paintings that Hopps recalls were moving "away from gestures, more toward Still . . . but not overall like Still."[10] Irwin recalls that it was very much about gesture, the authentic mark, of just trying to get it down without thinking too much about it.

Irwin's group of small "hand-held" paintings were a direct response to his March 1959 show at Ferus—a working critique of the Sawtelle and Zen paintings he'd seen together for the first time.

Untitled, ca. 1959-60
Oil on canvas in wood frame
11 5/8 x 11 1/2 inches
Collection of the artist

A lot of what I had been doing in those large gestural paintings . . . seemed to me afterwards as being not very controlled . . . . So I started out painting the same paintings on a very small scale, where I could really control every gesture, so that each one was very much an intended thing.[11]

Made between the fall of 1959 and the spring of 1960, the hand-held paintings quite literally combined the gestural performance of Irwin's large Zen paintings and the more deliberate procedures of the Pick-up Sticks paintings to follow.

"Made," because issues of presentation, including custom frames, approached parity with "painting," as Irwin extended the control issue beyond himself to circumstances of reception by the viewer. The hand-helds began to redefine painting for him as a way of seeing—an occasion to focus one's attention.

Like the Sawtelle and Zen paintings, the hand-helds can be described as "linked solutions describing early and late stages of effort upon a problem."[12] Painted within months of one another in a small apartment,[13] usually in a single session, they appear to divide into two distinct groups. The so-called early hand-helds are smaller and more colorful; dominant hues range from yellows and reds to earth tones, dark blues, blue-grays, blue-greens passing black. The larger late hand-helds (about thirteen to twenty-one inches) feature lighter neutral colors, from pale grays to ochres, mixed with white and black, animated by traces of brighter blues, greens, reds—often as revealed letters and symbols drawn into wet paint. Primarily small brushes were used in the early paintings, a mixture of brush and knife work in the late ones. At this time Irwin also began to take an interest in quality materials, in part from Kauffman's example, in part because on the smaller scale he could afford to.[14]

With an autodidact's zeal, Irwin supervised all details of the custom-made frames and backings—thick mouldings, tightly boxed right up to the edge to highlight textures and to encourage holding the paintings for close inspection when not placed on edge or flat on the table. (Grommets and a black cord on the backing permitted wall hanging.) Irwin's attention to detail extended to pairing individual paintings with different hardwoods to complement their color, and rubbing skin oils from his hands and face to give the wood a subtle patina front and back.[15]

The early hand-helds are fastidious, successive accretions of pigments, swirled and shaped into suggestive layers of color and texture, some gestures carrying out to the edges. Cast shadows and the frequently metallic sheen of thirty-year-old paint confer on the darker paintings an ambiguous presence: here, yet distant. In contrast, some of the larger hand-helds have the intimacy of still-life painting; the facture and centered shapes in one *Lucky U* variation recall the work of Giorgio Morandi.

Both groups, however, function as conditional objects, subject to circumstance, inviting us to manipulate the painting, to control the light, to make of it a conscious, fluctuating experience. Irwin was still some years away, of course, from defining his activity in phenomenological terms. But the ramifications of what he was attempting with the hand-helds anticipate the experiential/perceptual issues in the line paintings.

Although Irwin's hand-helds were indeed experimental and intended "for his own research," he did exhibit them on at least four occasions: in March 1960 at UCLA (a single example, *Red Painting*); in his one-man show at Ferus in April, which was expanded into his first one-man museum show at the Pasadena Art Museum in mid-July; and, in August, his entry in the 1960 Annual Los Angeles and Vicinity exhibition: *Lucky U*.

At twenty-one inches square, this *Lucky U* (and the smaller Morandi-inspired painting of the same title discussed above), seem to have been hand-held variations of Irwin's much larger *The Lucky U* of 1959, the title likewise cut. The smaller *Lucky U* does not in fact resemble its large cousin, and the appearance of the version in the 1960 Annual is unknown. Their titles suggest, however, that Irwin had indeed "started out painting the same paintings on a very small scale"—that some hand-helds began as gestural riffs upon the Zen paintings, energized by reduction, focused by the frame.

Irwin's new hand-helds comprised his second solo show at Ferus in April;[16] many of these were shown again in mid-July at the Pasadena Art

Lucky U, 1960
Oil on canvas in wood frame
15 1/2 x 15 1/2 inches
Private collection, courtesy of
Joni Gordon, Newspace,
Los Angeles, and Adrienne Fish,
871 Fine Art, San Francisco

Lucky U, 1960
Back and sides of painting

Form for Tomorrow, 1960
Oil on canvas in wood frame
16 1/8 x 15 1/2 inches
Courtesy of Margo Leavin,
Los Angeles

Museum, in a show organized by Walter Hopps, whose plan was to bracket what he perceived as the two extremes of contemporary art in California: the lyrical, abstract side (Irwin) and the dark side, assemblage (Ed Kienholz).[17] The Pasadena exhibition was also a de facto retrospective of Irwin's "serious" work to date.[18] One reached the eighteen hand-helds through an adjoining gallery installed with six of Irwin's best Sawtelle and Zen paintings from his Ferus exhibition the year before. As though to underscore the dynamic between them, *Kanzan*, his largest painting ever, was centered on the axis wall.

The hand-helds appeared in public because Irwin had finished with them, probably by March 1960 when he left for Europe, considering them "too controlled, and therefore mannered." Nevertheless, the hand-helds taught Irwin to build upon questions—and contradictions—generated by his own work: this would become the heart of his future practice.

While driving through northern Italy in June with Bengston (who remembers going to the Venice Biennale), Irwin had the sudden insight that lines might be the way out of his imagery dilemma—that a line was the least referential kind of mark he could make without abandoning marks—and physical presence—altogether.

Most likely in July 1960, Irwin and Bengston found large cheap studio space on Pier Avenue, near the beach in Ocean Park, where Irwin moved quickly to exercise his newly won "control" by making larger paintings again—sixty-five by sixty-six inches—and to test his conviction that lines would be the least referential marks he could paint. Over some six months he made several of these transitional paintings, which he dubbed "Pick-up Sticks" because of the long, flowing, criss-crossed strokes.

Untitled, 1960
Oil on canvas in wood frame
15 3/16 x 15 3/16 inches
Collection of Roberta Neiman, Los Angeles

From compositions consisting of some forty to fifty lines he gradually worked down to seven or eight, ever straighter and more horizontal, with fewer short connective lines grounding the major strokes to the field and to one another. From there Irwin soon moved during the first months of 1961 into the four-line paintings and the end of his formal "reeducation."

The three known Pick-up Sticks paintings—*Ocean Park, Pier I,* and *Pier II*—are testament to a concerted effort to simplify and focus. Although reducing the number of linear strokes, Irwin seems to have developed some of them into complex forms in their own right, thereby contradicting his objective. At center in *Pier II,* for example, the irregular line not only has a distinct silhouette but it is further articulated with a glowing interior of white impasto slivered with red edges; in this context it reads not only as a distinct form, but as a veritable character with narrative implications. Tonally and texturally distinct, these "lines" in *Pier I* and *Pier II* reassert the colored field as ground, behind them. The overall effect, as Weschler has observed, is "to backslide"—in effect to return to relational, part-to-part scanning of the lines, "the way energy passed among them." As paintings they have undeniable presence; but they still read as pictures—as views of something exterior to themselves.

Least pictorial is *Ocean Park,* probably the earliest of the three known Pick-up Sticks and the most traditional in terms of organization and facture. It is least pictorial in part because of its opaque yellow ground which recedes only so far (a characteristic that Irwin would exploit in the late line paintings). Reinforced with wide zig-zag brushwork in the top third of the canvas—in a slightly acid, putty variation of that yellow—and other yellows worked into the deep cadmium red and bright green layers of superimposed "lines"—the net effect of the dominant yellow is to pull everything up close; the painting reads first as hue and texture, secondarily as "space." *Ocean Park* does remains "pictorial," a "still-life" perhaps, like some of the hand-helds. But as a much larger painting, this secondary illusion vanishes more easily than the atmospheric "landscape" of backlit lines in *Pier I* and *Pier II.*

To isolate the backgrounds in each Pick-up Sticks painting is to see intimations of later line paintings. As physical objects, however, they are a step back from the hand-helds, mounted on simple stretcher bars with one vertical brace; they display none of the exacting detail resumed with the late lines and dots, in which Irwin reasserts his preoccupation with finish front and back—reaffirming their transitional urgency. Perhaps even more than the hand-helds, the Pick-up Sticks functioned as personal research.[19]

Although Irwin was then beginning to work through issues related to his own painting, he was still very open to what was around him, still learning from other artists. In the Pick-up Sticks the most striking comparison is one of John Altoon's thick, richly colored paintings from 1956-57 (vertical in orientation but otherwise very similar in color and texture) and the work of Joan Mitchell, whose nature-inspired abstraction was shown regularly in Los Angeles, and like Altoon's, very much admired by Irwin.[20]

Ocean Park, ca. 1960-61
Oil on canvas
65 1/2 x 65 1/8 inches
Collection of the artist

Pier I, ca. 1960-61
Oil on canvas
65 1/2 x 65 1/8 inches
Collection of the artist

By the time of the early line paintings Irwin had begun to distance himself from his immediate surroundings, including contemporary painting, withdrawing into the studio, risking reinventing the wheel, as he put it, in order to discover his own vision, to understand his own perceptual faculties, to ground himself at that point in the making of his own work. To understand the necessity of this, for him, had been the point of his reeducation. Without this grounding, history—and other painting— was of little consequence.

Abstract Expressionism was many things to Irwin: an optics, a license to let go, a discipline—the means to reengage with his generation—and most important, the beginning of a self-critique and way of thinking. On another level it was a way of asserting his fundamental individuality, less as competitiveness (which he had in abundance) or intensity (which is still with him) but in the kind of ambition that inspired Barnett Newman to liken the vision demanded by painting—the vision to see a painting as it really is—as the means also to change the world.[21] It was a standard, but also a goal.

Notes

Irwin, 1955

1. Lawrence Weschler, *Seeing is Forgetting the Name of the Thing One Sees: A Life of Contemporary Artist Robert Irwin* (Berkeley and Los Angeles: University of California Press, 1982), p.160. (Hereafter, Weschler).

2. In conversation. In addition to two meetings, one in California in May and a second in New York in June 1992, the author conducted numerous telephone interviews with the artist between April 1992 and January 1993. For their help with this essay, thanks also to Eugenie Candau, Hal Glicksman, Henry T. Hopkins, Alberta Mayo, Dan Mills, and Gerald Nordland, as well as many others too numerous to list here. Weschler, p.28, raises the critical question about the artist's apparent lack of memory of his early life: "When Bob speaks of the 'charmed' nature of his early life, is this because he actually did experience a happy youth, or because he really was able to disregard whatever pain there was as it was happening, or because he's been able to disregard it since? One wonders, especially because of the starkness of the solitude this youth subsequently engendered. There is an irreducible mystery in all of this." Irwin's commitment to art as something life-enhancing has parallels to artists for whom art was first a personal and second a societal form of healing. On the relation of pleasure and healing, "as a practical regulator of states of crisis," see "Julia Kristeva," an interview with Alice Jardine in *Discourses: Conversations in Postmodern Art and Culture*, ed. Russell Ferguson, William Olander,

Marcia Tucker, and Karen Fiss (Cambridge, Mass: The MIT Press; and New York: The New Museum of Contemporary Art, 1990), p.87. See also Ellen Handler Spitz, *Art and Psyche: A Study in Psychoanalysis and Aesthetics* (New Haven, Conn.: Yale University Press, 1985), esp. pp.20, 43-46. Irwin's long-term effort now, over twenty years, to discuss his insights into perceptual behavior within the context of Western philosophy and science is directly related to his wish that what he has discovered for himself be accessible to anyone. Many of those experiences have counterparts in Zen, and a number of Irwin's students recall his teaching methods as analogous to those of Zen masters, a sharp word and leaving the room, etc. Zen for Irwin is a charged subject and in part because of its faddish aspects in the fifties and sixties he is understandably reluctant to identify with Zen practice. But it is clear that Irwin's introduction to Zen and his experience of it in all its serious and mock-serious manifestations with the other Ferus artists had a deep impact on his thinking. Intellection, of course, is the opposite of Zen's wordless intuition. For Irwin to discuss his thinking in terms of phenomenology, and later Hegel, Kant, Hume, Plato, and the pre-Socratic philosophers is not only, I believe, an effort, as he has said, to be understood within a Western framework. It is also his effort to shake off any single, dominant ideology, to insist on alternative discourse, to deny any one philosophy or method the control of his senses; to remain open to experience, as it is. (Which is also a way of Zen.)
3. Jeffrey Wechsler, *Abstract Expressionism, Other Dimensions: An Introduction to Small-scale Painterly Abstraction in America, 1940-1965* (New Brunswick, N.J.: Jane Voorhees Zimmerli Art Museum, Rutgers, 1989), questions whether mere size can define Abstract Expressionism as a style. His discussion of East Coast-West Coast dynamics, gendered clichés, and the disparagement of oriental aesthetic concepts such as "subtlety and refinement" are relevant to the reception of Irwin's later work in New York in 1964 and later. (Irwin's hand-helds are not mentioned).
4. See William Claxton and Hitoshi Namekata, *Jazz West Coast: Artwork of Pacific Jazz Records* (Tokyo: Bijutsu Shuppan-Sha, 1992), pp.51, 118, for front and back of Irwin's Chet Baker album cover (1955), a stylized trumpet with a bird in the upper right corner, perhaps a tribute to

Charlie Parker (died March 1955) with whom Baker got his start. Irwin did a second cover in 1959, *The Sound of Big-Band Jazz in Hi-fi* (WP 1257) with two stylized saxophones, p.50. John Altoon had done covers since the early 1950s in New York and made the connection for Irwin. Irwin's was the second of a "West Coast Artists Series" project to commission younger painters around L.A. Irwin's cover was reproduced in *Graphis* 13, no. 73 (September-October 1957) in Robert M. Jones, "Record Cover Designs," p.443, together with a Count Basie design by Andy Warhol. Irwin had met Baker and Gerry Mulligan in the early 1950s. Irwin's title for an early line painting, *Way Out West*, refers to Sonny Rollins's 1957 hit album of the same title. See Claxton, p.86, for the image. Compare, for example, references to jazz and jazz clubs in Brenda Richardson (with Mary Martha Ward), *Frank Stella: The Black Paintings* (Baltimore: Baltimore Museum of Art, 1976), pp.36, 58, 67 68, 71. This remains the best study of the contextual meaning of supposedly insignificant titles in recent abstract painting.
5. Interview, September 1992.
6. For example, see Betty Turnbull, *The Last Time I Saw Ferus, 1957-1966* (Newport Beach, Calif.: Newport Harbor Art Museum, 1976), James Monte, *Late Fifties at the Ferus* (Los Angeles: Los Angeles County Museum of Art, 1968), and Peter Plagens, *Sunshine Muse: Contemporary Art on the West Coast* (New York: Praeger, 1974).
7. Automobiles are usually cited in the evolution of the 1960s L.A. "finish-fetish" concern for surface and scrupulous detail, but Bengston and Kauffman, among others, stress the personal experience of making or handling ceramics. (Interviews). See also Bernard Pyron, "The Tao and Dada of Recent American Ceramic Art," *Artforum* 2, no. 9 (March 1964): 41-43; and John Coplans, *Abstract Expressionist Ceramics* (Irvine, Calif.: University of California, Irvine, 1966). Irwin says that he did not personally make any ceramics. But his experience of Zen tea bowls in Allen Lynch's ritual evenings was critical: Kauffman (Interview, September 1992) felt that the material—not the image—and the presentation, one bowl at a time, clearly had an impact on Irwin's subsequent practice.
8. Hopps (Interview, September 1992). Irwin (Interview, October 1992) recalls that he read all the Beckett he could find. *Evergreen Review* was

another source.

9. *Recent Paintings by Robert Irwin*, March 23 to April 18, 1959.

Clambering up the Cold Mountain path,
The Cold Mountain trail goes on and on:
The long gorge choked with scree and boulders,
The wild creek, the mist blurred grass.
The moss is slippery, though there's been no rain,
The pine sings, but there's no wind.

All I can say to those I meet:
"Try and make it to Cold Mountain."

Selected by the artist from "Twenty-Four Poems by Han-Shan," translated by Gary Snyder ["Gary Snyder: Cold Mountain Poems, 'Twenty-four poems by Han-shan'," *Evergreen Review* 2, no. 6 (Autumn 1958), pp. 69-80; the catalogue excerpt combines the first six lines of Snyder's poem no. 8 and the last two lines from the final poem in this selection, no. 24.]

Catalogue
1. *Sawtelle No. 3*, 1958
Oil On Canvas, 60" x 57"
2. *Sawtelle No. 4*, 1958
Oil On Canvas, 58" x 59"
3. *Sawtelle No. 9*, 1958
Oil On Canvas, 71" x 72"
4. *Sawtelle No. 11*, 1958
Oil On Canvas, 72" x 71"
5. *G. A. A.*, 1958
Oil On Canvas, 72" x 60"
6. *No. 17, Murphy*, 1958
Oil On Canvas, 66" x 66"
7. *No. 19, Wedlum*, 1958-1959
Oil On Canvas, 72" x 72"
8. *No. 21, Black Raku*, 1959
Oil On Canvas, 71" x 84"
9. *The Lucky U*, 1959
Oil On Canvas, 71" x 84"
10. *Kanzan*, 1959
Oil On Canvas, 83" x 121"
11. *Daisetz*, 1959
Oil On Canvas, 65" x 65"
12. *No. 24, Ten Bulls*, 1959
Oil On Canvas, 82" x 98"
13. *Six Collage Studies*, 1958

The titles include references to local landmarks, to Beckett, and to Zen.

10. Hopps, October 1992.
11. Weschler, p.57.
12. George Kubler, *The Shape of Time* (New Haven, Conn.: Yale University Press, 1962), p.35. Irwin's preference for designating his work as Early and Late and for open "groups" as opposed to closed "series," might be traceable to the wide reading of this book among artists in the early and mid-1960s.
Bengston recalls that "we never thought in terms of 'series' in those days; that came in with the art market: 'series' meant more money!"
13. Irwin believes that all the hand-helds were painted in one location, a "Hollywood-Venetian" apartment house in West Hollywood. He shared the small apartment with Billy Al Bengston, each taking a room. Ken Price remembers them there in late 1959, and early 1960, painting on easels where they lived, "right in their bedrooms: they painted like gentlemen in there, no paint on the floors." (Irwin says the place was all white, like a studio but with white carpets). Bengston recalls that they were making one painting at a time and "noodling around" waiting for them to dry, he working on his motorcycles, Irwin reading his racing sheet. Irwin says that the smaller hand-helds were in fact made in one session —they were, after all, gestural Abstract Expressionist paintings—because it was impossible to get back into it later. He believes that he did come back to some of the larger ones, however, so long as the paint was still wet enough to work. At the time Bengston was also painting small, thickly painted images of flags, stars, and hearts, edge to edge, with stripes and jazzy colors that the others in the group feel helped Irwin to loosen up his own color.
14. Around this time, when Irwin was also teaching at Chouinard, he began to learn about quality paints from Ted Gibson, whose art supply and frame store around the corner was apparently one of few sources for rag papers and imported pigments in L.A. Irwin credits Gibson with guiding him to new options. By the time of the Pick-up Sticks paintings, and even more intensely in the evolution from the early to late lines, Irwin spent considerable time working out a palette, of experimenting with paints from different manufacturers and coming to conclusions about those he preferred to use as he reduced that palette: Robersons Art Materials (London) for reds; Oudt-Hollandse

(Dreibergen) for earth colors; Lefebvre-Foinet (Matisse's supplier in Paris) for whites. Irwin observes that as he became more knowledgeable the materials in each group of paintings were progressively better.

15. Sid Zaro had a frame shop on Fairfax that Ferus artists used regularly. He recalls working closely with Irwin on the hand-helds, fabricating and assembling the frames to the artist's exacting specifications. Irwin selected various stock—walnut, maple, poplar—to complement the different tonalities of each painting. The one-and one-half inch mouldings were custom milled without a rabbet right to the edge and individually cut for each painting. Weschler, p.58, describes very well the lavish attention Irwin paid to the hand-helds, drawing the parallel to "hot rod aesthetics" in which every detail, seen and unseen, would be perfected with a "passionate concern for the consistency of the whole." He describes Irwin rubbing even the interior of the boxes and his disdain for "artificial products when polishing the wood frame, confining himself solely to the natural oils of his hands, his forehead, the sides of his nose and so forth." Zaro recalls Irwin using body oils to darken the wood but also that he, Zaro, stained others with lacquer or fast-drying stains, or sealed them with clear lacquer. Irwin thinks this could well have been the case, particularly with the larger hand-helds, allowing that there were limits to the oil he could rub off the sides of his nose.

16. We know little about the specific contents of Irwin's 1960 one-man show of his new hand-helds at Ferus (April 18-May 14). The simple announcement card, however, aptly organized the three typefaces at right angles to one another into one rectangular block (perhaps another allusion to Morandi). Irwin, in Europe since March, did not attend the opening.

17. Hopps, (Interview, September 1992). When one considers the hand-helds specifically, the lavish attention to every detail of their making, the special frames in complementary woods, rubbed with oils from the artist's face and hands, and the tongue-in-cheek titles referencing members of the gang (Big 'Blum,' and The Swinging 'Z,' owned by Irving Blum and Sid Zaro, respectively)—they emerge as real fetish objects, no less so than Kienholz's found-objects or even the boxes of Wallace Berman, artists with whom Irwin's work otherwise bears little if any comparison. It is odd work, embodying the full range of Irwin's agenda at the time, risking preciosity and even vulgarity to gain one's undivided attention.

18. The Pasadena checklist included lenders, and prices, which ranged from $300-650. 1. Murphy; 2. Lucky U (sic), Lent by Mrs. [Helen] Jacobs; 3. Untitled; 4. Kanzan; 5. G.A.A.; 6. Daisetzes (sic, Daisetz), Mr. Mitchell Wilder [then head of Chouinard]; 7. California's Finest; 8. The Swinging 'Z', Lent by Mr. Sid Zarro (sic, Zaro); 9. Untitled; 10. Big 'Blum', Lent by Mr. Irving Blum; 11. Mammoth Mountain; 12. Untitled; 13. Untitled, Lent by Mrs. Bobby Neiman; 14. Saltfish; 15. Untitled; 16. Drag Down Dreamsville; 17. Big White; 18. Untitled, Lent by Mr. and Mrs. Horace Baber; 19. Bauncy's 'B' (sic, Barney's 'B') [Barney's Beanery, the bar favored by the Ferus artists after the Lucky U]; Havenhurst, [Irwin's studio street], Lent by Dr. and Mrs. R. Bookman, 21. Untitled; 22. Challenger Deep, Lent Anonymously; 23. Ed, Mary and Claud, [Ed Kienholz, his first wife, and their dog]; 24 Kelly Buns, Lent by Mrs. Sadie (sic, Sayde) Moss.

19. Irwin does not recall if he ever showed the Pick-up Sticks at Ferus; Ocean Park was included in 1961 in "Pacific Profile of Young West Coast Painters," June 11-July 1961, at the Pasadena Art Museum. The Pasadena label dates Ocean Park to 1959, the catalogue to 1961. As an earlier painting in the group of 1960-61 would be closer. Others do recall seeing the Pick-up Sticks or "Zig-Zags" at Ferus, most likely in a group show.

20. Compare Altoon's Untitled, ca. 1956-57, illustrated in color in Jay Belloli, John Altoon: Twenty-five Paintings, 1957-1969 (Pasadena: Baxter Art Gallery, California Institute of Technology, 1984), cat. 1.

21. "Almost fifteen years ago Harold Rosenberg challenged me to explain what one of my paintings could possibly mean to the world. My answer was that if he and others could read it properly it would mean the end of all state capitalism and totalitarianism. That answer still goes." Barnett Newman, " 'Frontiers of Space' Interview [1962] with Dorothy Gees Seckler," reprinted in Barnett Newman: Selected Writings and Interviews, ed. John P. O'Neill, text and commentary by Mollie McNickle, intro. by Richard Shiff (New York: Knopf, 1990), pp.247-51.

Expression: Lines, Dots, Discs; Light

Jeremy Gilbert-Rolfe

In the 1960s artists ended to move away from the overt expressionism of the previous decade towards a concern with the morphology of the object, frequently with a view to expanding its identity and the limits of its address. The morphology of the object is the list of ingredients which constitute it as a thing, or more precisely as a system of some sort. In the case of the work of art, it is a thing which functions as a certain kind of sign, in that and also despite it, producing a certain kind of significance. It is in these terms that one would see the work of art as a combination of traces of activity performed and preserved in the interests of contemplation, as a specific presentation and rearrangement of the possible components of the object-as-sign, including emphasizing some and excluding others (i.e., redefinition through rearrangement), and as an analysis and use of the conventions of the object which permit it to function as both the meeting place and the producer of ideas and of an experiential effect.

The work that Robert Irwin made during that period certainly fits that general description. Beginning as painting and then extending the terms of painting into the disc, an object dependent on painting's conventional terminology (i.e., its identity as a cluster of conventions) but which is not a painting and is also not exactly an object, one finds in Irwin's work an extreme attentiveness to the material condition of the object. That this attentiveness amounts to fetishizing the work's finish is not quite the whole story. It is more germane that this attention is lavished on the piece in the interests of putting the act of looking at the core of one's encounter with the work.

On this last point it is worth remembering that both looking and reading come into play when one encounters objects, or alternatives to objects, meant to be primarily or exclusively aesthetic. This follows from what I've said to be a general interest in the morphology of the art object (or event) on the part of those who make art in the latter part of the twentieth century. The work is both an experience, to which one must in some sense surrender oneself, as it were, uncritically, and a text, a series of deployed conventions which invites decoding, i.e., which awaits a (critical) reader. The implication of this is that the work of art can only be uncritically experienced (seen) once it's been critically decoded (read). For example, no one unfamiliar with painting and its concerns at the time of Cézanne could claim to be able to perform that suspension of the will to interpret which contemplating the artist's work would imply. Such a viewer would have no idea of the context in which that contemplation was supposed to take place. Contemplation is not the same as bafflement, which is what would befall the viewer innocent of history. To be baffled is to be in a state where one struggles to figure out what it is one has encountered—how to read this

Members of the Ferus Gallery, ca. 1959. Left to right: Ed Kienholz (seated), Allen Lynch, John Altoon, Ed Moses, Billy Al Bengston, Robert Irwin, Craig Kauffman

thing, what is its language, what-ever am I looking at? To con-template is to know how to read the thing insofar as it can be read, and having reached that point—or at least having more or less acquired some sense of what reaching that point might be like—to be engaged in seeing what else it has to say to the viewer/reader who is prepared to be patient. This is not to say that contemplation may not yield baf-fling results, for to reach a point where one encounters that which is not a code, and is therefore not susceptible to being decoded, is to reach the limit of the express-ible. But one would not want to confuse where contemplation (looking closely but uncritically) begins with where it ends. For one thing it seldom either begins or ends in the same place.

"When art is dressed in the most threadbare cloth, we recognize it most clearly as art." [1]

A number of questions come to mind when one asks oneself how and why Irwin came to make the work of the sixties. The idea of looking closely at something made with the most limited means (a restrictive deployment of the object's conventionality) certainly had precedents in the general history of twentieth-century art, and, of course, before that. Constructivism is never far away, for example, when one finds the artwork's content identified with stripping the object bare. Nor, when the object in question is a painting, is Malevich (a Cubo-Futurist rather than a Constructivist). Nor, as John Coplans pointed out at the time these works were made, should one dis-count the indirect influence of Ad Reinhardt or Mark Rothko. [2] Irwin's line paintings, and the discs, may be located within that history of painting which one identifies with concepts like reduction—a tradition which holds that success requires the prior exclusion of the superfluous.

The 1960s saw the spread of a general presumption that reduction, in the sense of working with the least possible means from the beginning, had become a credible place from which to start. One has, with this presumption, moved from a notion of abstraction to one of nonrepresentation: the work is no longer a process in which

Billy Al Bengston, Craig Kauffman, and Robert Irwin, Santa Monica Canyon, California, early 1960s

something occurs in the search for some sort of essence, but is instead born pared down, and working with it proceeds from there. Paraphrasing Nietzsche, one may say artists now sought to begin with the threadbare, and maintain and develop it in its pared-down (actually, worn-down) clarity. One recalls Robert Ryman's answer when asked why he painted only white paintings (which are to him nothing of the sort). He replied that he wanted to see the painting naked, and to work with that.[3] Ryman's is a career which parallels Irwin's and to which I shall return.

Two questions, which are really three, come to mind when thinking of the origins and motives of Irwin's work of the sixties. These are the questions of the Los Angeles context, and the question of what was happening at that time in New York. The third question, implied by these two, would have to do with the rivalry between New York and Los Angeles. Or more properly between Los Angeles and New York, since it was L.A. artists who felt somehow left out, while New York artists didn't feel they had any rivals.

Talking to people who inhabited it, including Irwin himself, one gets the impression that the art world in L.A. in the sixties was small and united by stylistic assumptions which did not turn into shared formal or intellectual concerns. I mean by this that L.A. artists of the sixties were all quite involved in L.A. culture—itself expressible as a triad: the sun; the beach; the automobile—and this played a role in determining some aspects of their work, but that didn't by any means mean that what one made would ultimately bear any resemblance to that made by another.

Irwin's infatuation with the automobile, is, as they say, legendary. Its purest expression at the anecdotal level was his ejecting a putatively socially conscious New York critic from the car in which Irwin was driving him around, as a way of concluding an argument on the theme of the automobile as cultural object. Irwin, with the critic in tow, had dropped in on a young man who was restoring a car with great love and skill. An argument had subsequently ensued in which Irwin had suggested that what the kid was doing was a kind of folk art. The critic had insisted that, tainted by the inauthenticity of capitalist modes of production, it was nothing of the sort, comparing it unfavorably with the blankets made by the indigenous population on their reservations. Irwin retorted that such things were made for tourists, no longer had much connection to anything authentic, and asked his passenger to leave without giving him the option of remaining.

There's probably nothing like being stranded on the side of a freeway in Orange

County to encourage a renewed respect, or hatred, for the motor car. The level of passion suggested by this anecdote—even allowing for the singularly tiresome nature of that particular critic—suggests to me that the lessons learnt from restoring cars, an obsession of Irwin's youth, should probably not be underestimated. It seems correct for Lawrence Weschler to suggest that Irwin's belief that a poorly made stretcher would have a visible effect on the work, even though it itself would be invisible, is probably a conviction reinforced by, if not founded in, that experience.[4] Dave Hickey has made the point, in conversation, that the colors chosen by L.A. painters often reflect the color schemes offered contemporaneously by the automobile industry. While the relationship of Irwin's art to the art of automobile designers is in no sense as literal and direct as that, it may well be that the idea of perfectibility which is so important to his work and that of his Californian colleagues of the time has its origins in the possibility offered by the car, in a place where rust and rain are negligible concerns for the enthusiast of the automobile, as a movable painted surface—a curved and enveloping surface which one may in fact occupy in the sense of being contained by it.

Weschler records a conversation between Irwin and Frank Stella on the subject of the possibility of perfectibility which illustrates the difference between New York and Los Angeles in the sixties, when that difference is seen from the L.A. point of view. Stella asked Irwin why he took so much trouble rendering the edges of his paintings impeccable. Irwin asked him why he didn't: "Why *don't* you? How can you not?"[5] For Irwin, as he put it to me, the difference of opinion demonstrates that for Stella the painting is only that which takes place within the bounds of its surface, that what takes place beyond that is somehow not seen, perhaps as a result of the kind of capacity for focus and bracketing out which goes with living in New York. The point is particularly well-taken in that the conversation in question took place in the mid-sixties, when Stella was making octagonal canvases painted with metallic paint and with a hole in the middle, which therefore gave one an edge both within and without that paralleled the stripes out of which the painting's surface was made. Stella's reply was "It's not important."

To Irwin, it was and is very important, and why it should be tells one a great deal about his work. In terms of the New York-Los Angeles axis, when this is considered as a relationship made out of a failure to communicate, the anecdote sets a New York (in the person of Stella) which values the rough (the roughness of the edge turns out to be significant after all, i.e., it is being *seen*, or more exactly *read*, a displayed imperfection which is an important component of the work), the big, the striking, the language perhaps of the immediate in the sense of the provisional, against an L.A. (represented by Irwin) concerned with the perfected, which is by definition not rough and need not be big, an attitude certainly interested in the immediate, but in a version of immediacy which conceives of itself as timeless.

There is another big difference between Irwin's paintings of the sixties and Stella's, which has to do with the place of intuition in the work. In paintings such as *Crazy Otto* (1962), Irwin made decisions intuitively which a painter like Stella would have wanted to be in some way deductive—to use the term proposed by Michael Fried at the time—consequences of the way the work was made. Again, the only sixties artist who comes to mind as someone who was working at that time in a way comparable to Irwin's and who never precluded the option of the intuitive leap is Ryman.

If one looks at the two paintings of Irwin's I've just mentioned one sees how it could be that a preoccupation with an immediacy that could sustain a great deal of looking might establish a logical progression that would ultimately cause the artist to abandon the stretcher, the generically identifiable painting-as-an-object which stands for Painting. Irwin told me that from his point of view the "loss of the object" was "just the same thing" as the earlier elimination of the frame: painting doesn't die, but one may work one's way out of it.

Other writers, including Weschler, have found it worthwhile to interpret Irwin's work through the phenomenology of the French philosopher Maurice Merleau-Ponty.[6] It's with a view to taking what others have said a little further that I put him to work again here, and suggest that an analysis of, for example, *Crazy Otto*, could well begin with a quite literal reading of Merleau Ponty's idea that: "A painting makes its charm dwell from the start in a dreaming eternity where we easily rejoin it many centuries later, even without knowing the history of the dress, furnishings, utensils, and civilization whose stamp it bears."[7] It is perhaps worth noting, apropos a point made earlier concerning a possible difference between looking and reading, that in the next sentence he goes on to say: "Writing, on the contrary, relinquishes its most enduring meaning to us only through a precise history which we must have some knowledge of."[8]

Crazy Otto is a brownish-green painting. In the notes I made to myself when preparing to write this essay, I described it as olive but not olive. Measuring sixty-six by sixty-five inches it is neither large nor small, and on it are painted three blue horizontal lines, which aren't equidistant but are instead intuitively placed. Above these three lines, near the top, is a fourth, similarly located by intuition, also blue but more intensely so. It seemed to me that the top line is perhaps Cobalt Blue plus white, while the other three may be Cerulean Blue plus white. (Irwin couldn't remember).

The ground—for want of a better term with which to describe the predominant part, which has lines painted *on* it, of a painting otherwise concerned to frustrate or obviate the traditional organization of vision in painting into that between figure and ground—of *Crazy Otto* appears to be painted with a half-inch brush using two kinds of strokes, one horizontal and the other, crossing it, about five degrees off the horizontal. The surface extends around the edges of the stretcher, and there it seems to be painted with an up-and-down stroke rather than an horizontal one. At the same time the painting is framed in white Plexiglas, which leaves about half an inch of the edge exposed (the stretcher is a bit more than two inches deep). This framing seems to be an early expression of Irwin's desire to make the work continuous with the whiteness of the wall. Or more exactly to make its relationship with the wall less clearly a matter of the edge as the place where disjunction occurs. Coplans, with a touch of

conceivably unconscious paradox, writes that "Central to Irwin's art, it would appear, is the notion of dissolving boundaries."[9]

This idea is very important, even if Coplans expresses it in a way which begs the question of what happens to the idea of the "central" when it occurs in the course or context of boundary dissolution. As a theme in the work, the dissolution of boundaries, and also, I should have thought, the idea of dissolution within boundaries, accompanies, and eventually comes to be as important as, the idea of the very carefully painted and otherwise executed object as a precondition of work meant to be looked at for a very long time. Like the other paintings he made during this period and later, *Crazy Otto* is slightly higher than it is wide, to compensate for the distortion projected onto the object by human perception. Looking at the work—describing it to oneself, but then looking at it in the less analytical sense of staring at it, looking uncritically—one realizes that this is a use of a particular set of the elements which might define painting, but it is not a matter of being reduced to them, in the sense of a reduction which leaves something out. It's a matter of an object defined through a particular array of its conventional possibilities in order to focus on the art object as a kind of accompaniment to human perception which, as such, reflects back onto its perceiver. Which is to say that Irwin's work proposes a viewer consciously engaged in active seeing, where seeing is at once a matter of concentration and focus and at the same time intransitive and involuntary. The slight difference between the height and width, the similarly small but significant difference between the strokes which make up the ground, in *Crazy Otto* are instances of the sort of phenomena which we label "imperceptible" when we mean exactly the opposite.

The question becomes, then, what are these boundaries that Irwin seeks to dissolve? This question is conceivably more complicated than it might seem. Looking, when thought of as perception without interpretation, is, to return to Merleau-Ponty, a timeless rather than an historical activity. In the case of Irwin, it's an activity which takes place within the context of a definition of the art object as something at once complete in its simplification and which simultaneously conceives and presents the art object as a world in which *everything matters*. As such a world, it is an apparition, a dream-state, an ideal form (or "realization") of the material. Painting is itself the form in which division always took place within a continuous surface, i.e., through the agency of a context which in theory could allow for no division.

As Irwin's work evolves, after paintings like *Crazy Otto*, one finds, it seems to me, a methodical inquiry into boundaries that begins (and which is why I bring up the possibility of dissolution *within* boundaries) *inside* the painting.

I'm not sure, however, that "dissolution" is after all an entirely adequate description of what is involved. If it is dissolution, and there is a primary sense in which it is, then it is dissolution as a result of over-definition. Not entirely unlike the effect caused by shining such a bright light on an object that, in illuminating it, one almost causes it to disappear. Jacques Lacan, the psychoanalyst, has suggested that that is what analysis can do, might even be prone to do, and one can see how it would be an almost implicit result of seeking to *concentrate* on *dissolution*.

Jake Leg, 1962
Oil on canvas
66 x 65 inches
Collection of
Earl Lewis Goldberg,
Brentwood, California

Crazy Otto, 1962
Oil on canvas
66 x 65 inches
The Pace Gallery, New York

Matinee Idol, 1962
Oil on canvas
66 1/8 x 65 1/8 inches
The Museum of Contemporary Art, Los Angeles
Given in memory of Gene Burton by Laura-Lee and Robert Woods

Irwin moved forward by painting works such as *Untitled* (1963-64), in which an orange-yellow painting bears two horizontal lines, which are also orange-yellow. The lines are painted more thickly than the ground (which may have looked flatter when it was first applied, since it was painted with a palette knife and has had more than twenty-five years to settle in). I thought Irwin may have used masking tape when painting the lines, but he told me no, he never used masking tape, he doesn't like what it does to the edge (which is interesting with regard to his disagreement with Stella, and is simultaneously a quite dramatic departure from the aesthetics of the car culture) but that he had instead built it up with a knife. This image (apparition within the real) of an orange-yellow line laboriously but inexorably being made to separate itself from an orange-yellow field, like a plant growing but remaining the same color as the ground out of and upon which it grows, could be seen as one that reverses rather than realizes the idea of dissolution. This, however, is not the whole story. Their very separation underscores the similarities between the line and the field, namely that they are made of the same color and material, and would dissolve into one another were they not held apart by drawing, i.e., by the line that bounds the line.

This could be expressed as follows. In Irwin's *Untitled*, line emerges from the field by itself being first inscribed by a line, because the lines in the painting are in effect long rectangles bounded by a line which must be both visible and invisible if *the* lines are to be seen as lines. This visibility/invisibility (which might be better expressed the other way around, since its primary goal is to be invisible) of the line which bounds *the* line, which is "really" a long rectangle, is enhanced and also reduced as it turns into what is actually the shallow walls of a relief. It is enhanced in that it's transformed from an abstraction into a wall—an edge, a facet of a thing, as opposed to a division, which is to say, an absence. And reduced in that it thus becomes the support for a surface rather than a border (a dividing line which limits the line it engenders, a line that traces a division which *sub*divides the painting as a whole) around an interior. A surface which is applied, moreover, by layering rather than filling in, i.e., a surface which is itself the trace of the continual repetition of a line. A line which moves across the field from which the line which bounds it, its edge, separates it in order to keep it connected. In Martin Heidegger's essay on van Gogh, "The Origin of the Work of Art," and in Jacques Derrida's commentary on it and its own origins, one reads about line as a void bounded by edges which it holds together. Irwin's line could almost be seen as the inverse of this. Line not as a depth but as a relief which both enhances and reduces, holds at a distance rather than holding together, its edges.[10] In this matter of the imperceptible as the object of a conscious perception, and of the line which brings into being the line (leaving aside the question of the relationship, within this, between the line that bounds and the layering which, through repeating the form of a line, also brings the same one into being as is engendered by the boundary which "places" it on the surface) one cannot move on without recourse to Merleau-Ponty, and to the similarity which emerges here

Untitled, 1962-63
Oil on canvas
82 1/2 x 84 1/2 inches
Norton Simon Museum,
Pasadena
Gift of the artist, 1969

Untitled, 1963-64
Oil on canvas
82 1/2 x 84 1/2 inches
Collection of Arne and Milly Glimcher, New York

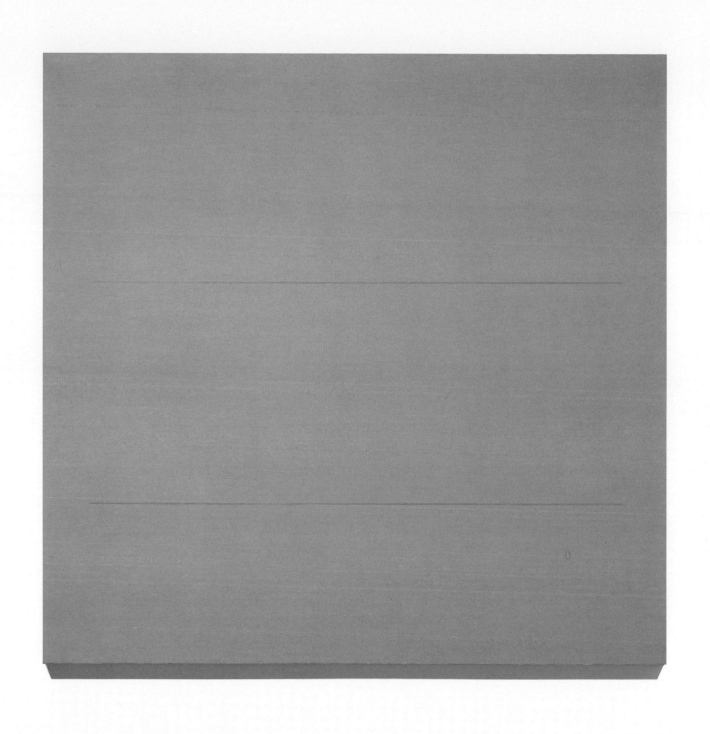

Untitled, 1962-64
Oil on canvas
82 1/2 x 84 1/2 inches
Collection of Edward and Melinda Wortz, Pasadena

between drawing and language: "Language is obscure in terms of its function, which is to render everything else clear. It cannot be observed or grasped directly; it can only be exercised."[11]

It is because of its articulation of the way in which, in painting, continuity and separation are functions of the same surface (as they are, in language, two sides of the same coin), that I see such works as *Untitled* as leading towards the discs. In the earlier group, which includes *Crazy Otto*, the relation of the work to the viewer, and to the wall, and to the question of what is going to constitute a painting, is presented as it were schematically: "human" scale; intuition; line and field; the idea of the meticulous as a prerequisite for concentration. With works such as *Untitled*, Irwin begins to move rapidly towards a dissolution of the surface and to an explicit investigation into the relationship of the art object to the idea and actuality of light.

In a brilliant essay on Irwin's painting Phillip Leider described the work of the mid-sixties as taking two risks, the first that of "losing presence as an art object for the sake of gaining presence as art," while "the second risk involves the reintroduction of an ambiguous, atmospheric space, which modernist painting has . . . been at pains to banish in the interests of non-illusionism."[12]

What is being described here is the parallel development of the work and its surface. As its edges become curved, complicating and eliding the relationship between the work and what is behind and therefore in front of it (its relationship to the wall being what conditions its relationship to the viewer), so too the surface itself becomes, as Leider puts it, "ambiguous" and "atmospheric."

In other words, as the relationship between the work and the world becomes more fully articulated, and incidentally but inevitably begins more explicitly to involve the light which illuminates it, the surface of the work becomes more elaborate, inviting an even closer scrutiny (or gazing) than before. Merleau-Ponty describes the landscape in Cézanne as both enveloping and curving away from the painter.[13] As the object turns into one in which it is possible for Irwin to subdue or elide the edge, the work moves away from the simultaneity of the canvas as a rectangle standing in an absolute opposition to the unbounded space of the rest of the world. It itself becomes the place of a movement, or of movements.

Frank Gehry, who knew Irwin and the rest of the Ferus artists in the period under discussion here, told me two things about the work and its context which are, I think, to the point. One is that Irwin used to talk about Georges Seurat. Seurat, in making the Impressionist analysis of atmosphere systematic, does I think provide a helpful point of reference and precedent for the pink and green dots which make up the surface of *Untitled* (ca. 1964-66). Seurat provides one with the idea of atmosphere as a kind of order but also—a tendency confirmed in Irwin's work—of order expressed as molecular repetition being inevitably perceived as atmospheric.

The other thing that Gehry told me has a more oblique relevance. Gehry described John Altoon, a central figure amongst the Ferus group (who died prematurely), as a kind of living muscle, pure reflex, capable of exploding into amazing

Untitled, ca. 1964-66
Oil on canvas on shaped
wood veneer frame
82 1/2 x 84 1/2 inches
Collection of Edward and
Melinda Wortz, Pasadena

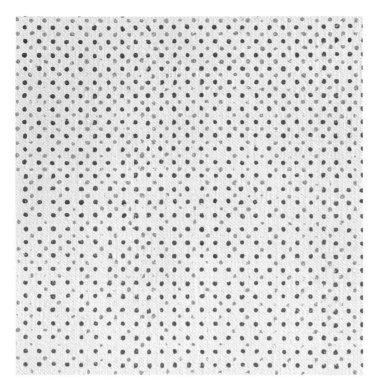

Detail of
Untitled,
(page 107)

painting and drawing but without conscious thought. This image seems strangely evocative of the kind of movement which enters into Irwin's work by the mid-sixties. Movement within and without the object, the object as a focus of movement, calling forth, I suggest, a viewer, a thinking subject, conceived not in terms of an absolute disjunction—the self-contained body posited by the flat rectangle which, returning the gaze that activates it, confirms in its simultaneity an idea of absolute presence—but as a zone or combination of movements.

In *Untitled* (ca. 1964-66), it's hard to tell where the curvature of the surface starts, i.e., where the flat part at the center begins to curve. As one moves towards the periphery of the disc the alternation of pink and green dots gives way to dots which are just green. The handmade quality of these works is, by the way, underscored when one looks closely at these dots. They're very unevenly painted, getting paler in some places and thicker and more intense in others.

But what one ends up wondering is whether these works are really about incorporating the edge into the painting, as Leider suggests, or whether they're about obviating the edge, using light and curvature, and also perhaps the idea of weightlessness, to propose a kind of continuity in which the edge becomes a transition rather than a rupture. It's almost possible to make the case that the center of the painting refers not so much to the rectilinearity of the stretcher as to the curvature of the edge and, in that, to the meeting of surface and light. One knows that Irwin spent a lot of time adjusting the color of the walls in front of which these works hung, painting out shadows, attempting to bounce light off the floor, as well as painting the backs of them white in an attempt to minimize the shadows they cast. Ideally he would prefer them to be seen only in natural light, which casts far less shadow than does artificial illumination.

Light facilitates perception but cannot itself be perceived except as a source— that which emanates light and therefore is itself not light—or through that which it lights up. It is, then, that which makes the visible possible but is not visible itself. Seeking to theorize a linking up between language and perception (the mutual alienation of which is, for example, the theme of the essay by Heidegger mentioned earlier), Merleau-Ponty was fascinated by the fact that seeing is done by two eyes, themselves accompanied by two hands. Relating tactility to vision, he talks of three kinds of touching: touching surfaces; being touched; and one hand touching the other, this last being an example of the kind of consciously perceiving subject said here to be implicit in Irwin's endeavor. He goes on to say:

> At the frontier of the mute or solipsist world where . . . my visible is confirmed as an exemplar of a universal visibility, we reach a second or figurative meaning of vision . . . which will be mind or thought. But the factual presence of other bodies could not produce thought or the idea if its seed were not in my own body. Thought is a relationship with oneself and with the world as well as a relationship with the other; hence it is established in the three dimensions at the same time. And it must be brought to appear directly in the infrastructure of vision.[14]

Irwin's work of the sixties realizes a certain possibility inherent in the art object: not the blurring of distinctions but their hyperdefinition. Hilton Kramer, the former art critic of *The New York Times*, once stood in front of an Irwin for half an hour and then asked if he could see a piece of work. He didn't realize that he was already looking at one. Whether this resulted from an innocence of art history or from reluctance (or innate inability) to look, it is testimony to the kind of hyperdefinition involved. It's a hyperdefinition which comes from fully illuminating the threadbare. Back in the sixties an (unsigned) piece on Irwin in *Art in America* commented on one of his works occupying a whole wall. Others have similarly established that each of their works requires a wall to itself: one work; one wall; one viewer (Ryman comes to mind, but it's the sort of thing that is bound to have been done by several people at once, all of whom think they did it first). This is a principle of reflexivity fundamental to what the work tells us. It isn't a matter of eroding boundaries, it's an affair of connecting, and of connection as envelopment. The work activates the space which contains it in a way which raises the question of what is activating what, within this envelope of light which also contains the viewer, drawn to the work in order to be redrawn by it, once there denied the kind of discrete separation from the world of things offered by more self-enclosed works of art. What happens in the work can only happen within my own field of vision, which I can no longer stand outside of, obliged as I am to see myself see, conscious of sharing the light of which the work ambiguously, which is to say, with hyperclarity, partakes. If Ryman turns out to be the painter who reactivated the object by bringing it as close as possible to the whiteness of the wall, Irwin is the artist who reactivated it by bringing it close to the whiteness of light (as opposed to paint), the disembodied force on which appearance depends.

I've made quite a lot of the uncanny parallel between Irwin's evolution and Merleau-Ponty's phenomenology. After Merleau-Ponty, philosophy gave up the attempt at reconciliation between language and perception, and there are signs that he himself was heading in the same direction, having literally worked his way through the problem without resolving it. In a manner that's not all that different Irwin, after making the works I've touched on here, increasingly reduced the physicality of the object in the interests of a more incorporeal envelopment. But Irwin's work of the sixties, even as it represents a stage of a still evolving inquiry, remains vital in its attempt to reconcile the object (the visible) with what makes it visible. Irwin took the possibility of making visible the art work's continuity with all that it is not to a level of realization where his achievement affects our understanding of all art, before, around, and after it. It has been suggested that the oval stretchers of the Analytic Cubist still life achieved that shape because the axiality of Cubist composition made it hard to deal with the four corners of the painting. In Irwin, the rectangle had to become a disc, not in order to dissolve its relationship with the wall, but in order to detach itself from the wall and propose another relationship to the curvature of vision and of the world.

John Baldessari once said to me that he thought that the L.A. artists of the sixties were able to do what they did because they didn't live in New York and therefore didn't know what they were supposed to be able to do and not do. Not unlike, I suppose, Kant being able to get away with ideas like that because he was after all stuck all the way over there in Koenigsberg. That L.A. is, perhaps, no more. In the work of Irwin (and, to be sure, of others, including Baldessari) it produced an art of international significance. Not bad for a car culture, when you come to think of it.

Notes

1. Frederick Nietzsche, *Human, All Too Human: A Book for Free Spirits* (Aphorism 179), trans. Marion Faber with Stephen Lehman (Lincoln, Nebr.: University of Nebraska, 1984), p.119.

2. John Coplans, "Robert Irwin," in *Robert Irwin* (New York: The Jewish Museum, 1968), unpag.

3. Jeremy Gilbert-Rolfe, "Appreciating Ryman," *Arts Magazine* 50, no. 4 (December 1975): 70-73.

4. Lawrence Weschler, *Seeing is Forgetting the Name of the Thing One Sees: A Life of Contemporary Artist Robert Irwin* (Berkeley and Los Angeles: University of California Press, 1982), pp.58-59.

5. Ibid., p.78.

6. Ibid., see p.179.

7. Maurice Merleau-Ponty, "Indirect Language and the Voices of Silence," in *Signs*, trans. and intro. Richard C. McLeary (Evanston, Ill.: Northwestern University Press, 1964), p.80.

8. Ibid.

9. Coplans, "Robert Irwin," in *Robert Irwin*, unpag.

10. Martin Heidegger, "The Origin of the Work of Art," Essay II of *Poetry, Language, Thought*, trans. and intro. by Martin Hofstater (New York: Harper & Row, 1975), pp.15-88; Jacques Derrida, *The Truth in Painting*, trans. Geoff Bennington and Ian McLeod (Chicago: University of Chicago Press, 1987), pp.255-382. For a further discussion of this relationship the reader may also be interested in Jeremy Gilbert-Rolfe, "Barthes's Challenge, Derrida's Truth," *Arts Magazine* 63, no. 8 (April 1989): 25-28.

11. Maurice Merleau-Ponty, *Consciousness and the Acquisition of Language*, trans. Hugh Silverman (Evanston, Ill.: Northwestern University Press, 1973), p.6.

12. Phillip Leider, *Robert Irwin* (Los Angeles: Los Angeles County Museum of Art, 1966), p.4.

13. Merleau-Ponty, "Cézanne's Doubt," in *Sense and Non-Sense*, trans. Hubert L. Dreyfus and Patricia Allen Dreyfus (Evanston, Ill.: Northwestern University Press, 1964), p.14.

14. Merleau-Ponty, *The Visible and the Invisible*, ed. Claude Lefort, trans. Alphonso Lingin (Evanston, Ill.: Northwestern University Press, 1968), p.145.

Robert Irwin, 1960s

The Architecture of Perception

Klaus Kertess

Robert Irwin spent most of a major decade of his career (the 1970s) working hard to leave almost nothing and no thing behind. If Gertrude Stein was obsessed with thingness (of her words—their sound and their becoming what they named), Irwin is obsessed with the atomization of thingness. Sometime around the date of Irwin's birth, Stein cantankerously complained about a town in Irwin's native state that "there is no there there." Irwin, however, in more celebratory cantankerousness, might well tell us that "there is no there there until you see there there." Irwin's "there" is all lightness and light; its primary boundaries are defined not by materiality but by the conditions of the viewer's aesthetic perception. He dissolved the object in the subject.

During the 1970s, Irwin's "there" might take place anywhere; but its most frequent location was within the confines of art museums. He did not add objects to a space: rather, he caused changes, often barely noticeable, in the visual climate of the space itself—something like moving Wichita's light to Omaha. He choreographed the given light and volume so that the space itself became a pedestal for thought. Now, of course, virtually all of these "theres" have been returned to their pre-Irwinian state; and there no longer requires quotation marks.

Given the extremely high degree of responsibility Irwin's work requires of the viewer and given the fact that almost none of his work done in the seventies remains, I the writer and you the reader now run the risk of permitting research to replace the primacy of visual perception which is the very issue his art is all about. Irwin's own articulateness and clarity about perception, helpful as it is, can engender further risk (he himself has become the major archaeologist of his lost culture). As ineluctable as the challenging logic of his work often seems, it can not be forgotten, or too often stated, that the analytical acuteness of Irwin's art is given non-verbal and intuitive presence by both his unique, personal sensibility (its willed depersonalization being part of it) and by his highly developed sense of visual rightness. The success of his dematerialization of art's conventional objecthood depends upon his ability to manipulate and activate scale, volume, light, and line into a potentially compelling relationship with the viewer.

Since I cannot re-view what I am writing about, this essay is dependent upon the vagaries of my memories of the not-so-immediate past, my reading, and my recent conversation with Irwin. Like most New Yorkers, my primary impression of Irwin's art was formed by his disc paintings done in the 1960s and shown at The Pace Gallery. Irwin was one of the few artists from the West Coast who became an exception to the New York art scene's prevailing conviction that Los Angeles was defined

Scrim Hall, 1988
(one of a series of transient
campus markings)
Rice University, Houston

113

by Hollywood and the Beach Boys. His conceptual rigor and astuteness, as well as the cool neutrality of his art's surfaces, were compatible with much of the art that was being made in New York in the sixties and early seventies; but the delicate vaporescence that has enlivened so much of his work proved problematic to many of us who were inured to the vague notions of "toughness" that had been called upon to validate so much of American art since the 1950s. Happily I (and many others) learned to give in. If there were any doubts about the scope and complexity of Irwin's undertaking, they were dispelled by the works he created in the seventies.

"Wrastle" and "breaking the frame" are two of the leitmotivs of Irwin's conversation. "Wrastle" lets you know that the methodical precision and seeming step-by-step certainty of Irwin's development have been fraught with trial, error, and uncertainty. "Breaking the frame" (literally and conceptually) might well be the subtitle of everything he has done. The rejection of pictorial illusion, bounded form, and hierarchical composition that was initiated by the Abstract Expressionists and then coolly regimented and further objectified, first by Jasper Johns in the mid-fifties, then by

Untitled, ca. 1966-67
Sprayed acrylic lacquer on
shaped aluminum
60 inches diameter
Collection of the artist

Kertess

Untitled, ca. 1966-67
Sprayed acrylic lacquer
on shaped aluminum
60 inches diameter
Collection of the artist

Frank Stella, was critical to Irwin as well. But, unlike Stella and the Minimalists of the sixties whose painting configurations are interdependent and coextensive with the shape and materiality of their support, Irwin sought to break the frame of the support, in order to make the painting not only more interactive with the space it is in but coextensive with it. Painting's reification was a logical step in the flight from illusion; and, for Irwin, the next step was the dissolution of the object and its dispersion in the viewer's field of vision. His disc paintings (ca. 1966-69) achieved a lyric interplay and co-identity of painting and ambient space, shadow and materiality, real light and painted light. The shadows thrown by the painted disc were as carefully planned and visually critical and imposing as the surface actually painted. Virtual objecthood now became virtual illusion. The dematerialization of the wall into a diaphanous suffusion of light notwithstanding, the central disc was still recognizable as painting and maintained a centered locus and focus within the space of the wall from which it projected out from. How to further diffuse objecthood and bring the experience still more into the space beyond?

Untitled, ca. 1966-67
Acrylic lacquer on formed acrylic plastic
54 inches diameter
Collection of the artist

Untitled, 1967-68
Acrylic lacquer on formed acrylic plastic
54 inches diameter
Norton Simon Museum, Pasadena
Fellows Acquisition Fund, 1969

In 1969, Irwin experimented with transparency, first with an eight-foot-square sheet of glass, generously curved at the bottom and more tightly curved at the top, then with two cast acrylic, columnar prisms, one winglike, one triangulated. The former prism rose to thirty-two feet (the third largest optical instrument ever made and the largest piece of acrylic ever fabricated in one piece). The curved and/or angled transparency of these pieces subtly warped the viewer's field of vision and cast reflections that ranged from rainbow amorphousness to radiant, straight lines, depending on shifts in light and viewing position—somewhat like being inside a quiet kaleidoscope. The near invisibility of these works and the heightened interactiveness of viewer and viewed was what Irwin was after. However, the glass piece was precariously dangerous (it was never shown publicly) and the high-tech prisms were cumbersome and costly—also a bit tricky, and Irwin is almost never tricky or theatrical. The space activation was still reliant on a discrete object, and a precious one at that. What was needed was a more flexible, low-profile material that could move space and light.

In the same year, Irwin also experimented with a variety of rented and borrowed lights used in commercial display, the theater, etc., in a twenty-by-twenty-by-twelve-foot room he set up next to his studio (he curved all the corners to facilitate the spread of light and to minimize the shadows). Here, he came to more fully understand the individual color and intensity of electric light that he had already begun to manipulate in the disc paintings.

In 1970, Irwin went to Amsterdam for an exhibition at the Stedelijk Museum. While there, he became increasingly aware of the transparent curtain material that screened so many Dutch windows. The near anonymity of its gridded weave and its semi-glossy, slippery surface, as well as the fact that it was made in the uncustomarily wide width of fourteen feet, gave it the potential to become a neutral yet dynamic visual lubricant for Irwin's desires. It gave him the means for an overall diffusion of light and the ability to move space along. This unobtrusive scrim material became a major agent in Irwin's quest for non-objectness in the seventies; the haze of light of the disc paintings could now be extended into a flat, porous plane defined by and redefining the volume and light of the space it was stretched across. It could help turn the entire room into a view. Irwin was now ready to leave his studio and make works directly in and responsive to the spaces he was asked to exhibit in. Not long after his return from Holland, Jenny Licht, then a curator at New York's Museum of Modern Art, offered him a space in which to test out his new ideas.

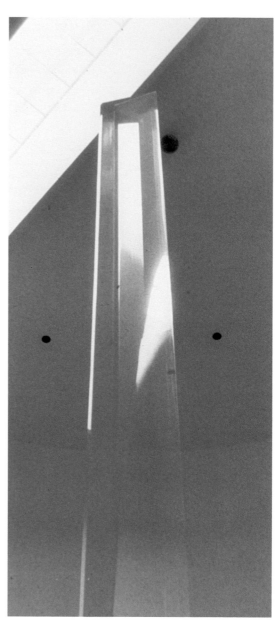

Cast acrylic column installed in the artist's studio, Venice, California, 1970

The room he was given to work with was an awkward alcove to the left of the space in which Brancusi sculptures were then exhibited; two avatars of purity (Brancusi of idealized form, Irwin of phenomenology) were now to enter into dialogue. Irwin set about activating the light and volume of the space. He cleaned the slotted skylight that ran the length of the ceiling (some three feet wide and deep) so that the light on the Brancusis fell in more perceptible bands. The other light in the room emanated from eight eight-foot-long fluorescent tubes that were covered by a strainer. Irwin changed the fixtures, making every other one different, alternating hot and cool. When these lights were covered by the egg-crate-like grid of the strainer, the light fell on the wall in fractured bands of warm and cool. The viewer entered the room through a floor to ceiling opening, not even noticing at first that the volume had been divided in two by a plane of scrim (some ten feet from the ground), making the light above brighter than the soft, hazy light below. Irwin was bothered by what he calls the "fatness" of the walls and by the fact that they were slightly bowed—they had a kind of dumb inertness that weighted the room and slowed down the eye. He lightened the walls by putting up wall-to-wall lines of stainless steel wire (about seven feet from the ground) and painted the wire white where it joined the walls. The resulting line could be seen but not visually held or anchored.

The room at the Modern had a kind of buzz that seemed almost subliminal. Something totally visual that eluded full verbalization, something more like what happens in front of a successful painting than in a nondescript architectural space was going on. The self-effacing manipulations of light, line, and volume that were once framed by painting's support now became congruent with the space for viewing. The eye was kept in constant motion; the reflexive perception of spatial relations was challenged. The viewer, if engaged, had to slowly question not what but how he or she saw —how he or she thought, where conscious perception met reflexive perception, what art was.

Irwin's means (but not his ends) are so unremarkable that many of his works executed in the seventies, like the one at the Modern, easily went unnoticed. Indeed, without the label declaring its artness (a label Irwin paid a student to remove every day and which the staff dutifully rehung), one might easily have passed by. I myself went in and got a subtle surprise but only learned of the light and light fixture changes in recent conversation with the artist. I now mostly remember being alternately entranced and perplexed by the glistening line I couldn't place. Depending upon cultural orientation, one could say Irwin has either a Zen or Classical bent for low-key coolness and discipline. His art is never confrontational, always willing to engage. Its challenge is quiet but forceful. His art exists somewhere between seduction and subversion, serenity and vertigo.

I linger over the work at the Modern, here, because I remember it. Not all of Irwin's subsequent pieces were quite so invisible. Some became more sculptural. He never had a preconceived blueprint for any of these works. They always evolved their diffused focus out of his highly tuned and centered focus on the character of the

space with which he was involved. Who else would become hyper-conscious of a wall's thickness? His hard-won mastery of scale and light as well as his overriding need for a stringent but elegant economy of means saw him through the seventies as they had seen him through the sixties.

Irwin's space-responsiveness took on a variety of manifestations. Some, like the project at the Modern, activated the preexistent qualities of the space, leaving it seemingly unchanged but elusively energized. Others, like the project done in 1983 for the Old Post Office in Washington, D.C., refocused the space. There, the vast atrium was articulated with a floating grid made up of rectangular panels of white screening. The grid organized the light into a shimmering play of translucency and transparency between the floating planes of the screens and the eight hundred windows that faced into the previous void of the atrium. The windows were now seen in a new light and space; they were given a real view. Something like an airborne Mondrian is going on here.

48 Shadow Planes, 1983
Old Post Office Atrium,
Washington, D.C.

Elsewhere, Irwin, with the subtlest of means, might intervene on the architecture's behalf. At Chicago's Museum of Contemporary Art in 1975, an awkwardly stranded pole in the middle of a room with only three walls was given a columnar dignity and a palpable centrality when Irwin closed the open rectangle formed by the black line of the baseboard. He extended a piece of black tape across the floor, connecting the two parallel walls. A simple, single line not only gave the desired closure to the space but tripped the unconscious reflexes of the viewers, many of whom found it difficult to cross the line. A piece of tape drew the line between reflex and conscious perception.

Still elsewhere, in what he referred to as "Spatial Drawing," Irwin gave dynamically spatial definition to the visually hidden structure of the space. At the University Art Museum, in Berkeley, California (1979), Irwin suspended fluorescent fixtures on three levels that corresponded to the brutish and apparently confused multi-levels of the space. The stacked planes ascended to an equilateral triangle at the center of the museum space and gave it a soaring and sorely needed visual logic.

Always Irwin's means were congruent with the space they activated, never did they coalesce into anything like a discrete object. The object was dissolved in the energies that catalyzed changes in and challenges to conventional perception. Irwin was neither the only nor the first artist to seek non-objecthood. In the late 1960s and

Black Line Volume
Installation, 1975-76
Museum of Contemporary Art,
Chicago

Three-Plane Triangulation,
1979
University Art Museum,
University of California,
Berkeley

early 1970s, a high moment of sculptural ferment saw the likes of Barry Le Va scattering felt and ball bearings across the floor (1966), Richard Serra flinging melted lead against the wall (1968), and Bruce Nauman quite literally making the viewer's viewing himself or herself the subject and the object of his art (*Live Taped Video Corner*, 1969-70). Irwin and these artists, like their modernist forebears, still believed strongly that inquiry was the central task of art. They made art more openly and dynamically contingent upon the viewer and upon the space it was viewed in. While Serra, Le Va, and others focused on the process of making and how the inherent nature of their generally malleable materials interacted with gravity and the physical boundaries of the containing space, Irwin focused on the space itself. His materials did not so much impinge upon the space as they became homogenized with it. His presence as an agent of making was purposefully suppressed.

The instances of Irwin's art here mentioned were mostly created within museums. And, during the seventies, that was where Irwin's work was most often seen. He could not support himself with his work (non-objecthood and livelihood are in inverse pro-

Slant Light Volume, 1971
Synthetic scrim, wooden frame,
double-stripped fluorescent lights, floodlights
96 x 564 inches (dimensions variable)
Walker Art Center, Minneapolis
Gift of the artist, 1971

Pure Space, 1990

The Museum of Contemporary Art, Los Angeles

portion to each other), but he was highly valued critically and museologically. In 1977, on the occasion of his exhibition at the Whitney Museum in New York, Irwin set about breaking the frame of the museum context and further begging the questions, what is art and where is it?

Irwin manipulated the volume and light of the Whitney's fourth floor in a manner related to his earlier installation at the Modern. The piece responded to the black plane of the floor and the open grid of the ceiling and incorporated a space-defining line on the walls. Parallels for these three elements (dark plane, grid, and volume-enclosing line) were then sought outside of the safe home of the museum and were incorporated in two sets of pieces, one fabricated, one found, in urban space. The first set included a black plane painted in the intersection of 42nd Street and Fifth Avenue, a black wire line circumscribing a rectangle that was drawn between the two lower, subsidiary towers of the World Trade Center; and a laser-drawn grid between 47th Street and 57th Street, on Park Avenue (due to lack of funds, this laser work could not be executed). Without the filtering focus of the museum context, the two executed pieces were readily confused with a variety of functional purposes (electrical wiring, traffic control, etc.) and could easily be absorbed by the cacophony of New York's preexistent grid. The risk to art's autonomy was further escalated in the second set of pieces, in which the fabrication of art was dispensed with. Irwin simply identified three situations: the full length of Park Avenue with its rectangular alternations of dark plane and light plane, the mercury vapor line extending around Central Park that had been installed by the city for its own purposes, and the entire grid of the Island of Manhattan. Not readymade objects *à la* Duchamp, the function of which changes from utilitarian to aesthetic as their context changes with their framing in a space dedicated to the aesthetic—but, rather, readymade situations precariously left in place and framed only by the aesthetic intention of the artist. Artness is now fully and solely dependent upon the fragile unwritten contract between artist and viewer.

While not the last of Irwin's galvanizations of existent light and space, these were the most extreme—a *reductio ad absurdum* or *cogito ergo sum* of aesthetic inquiry. He had brought his art to zero; having broken both the frame of the object and the frame of its context, his intentions merged with the flow of the quotidian. Having gone this far, he now felt empowered to employ anything at all in his celebration of perception—birds, rose-colored glass, grass-covered mounds, chainlink fencing, whatever might make the viewer more aware of his or her own acts of perception reflective of the place, space, and situation in the world shared with Irwin.

Irwin's 1970s are mostly a memory now; a memory of rigorous logic transformed into buoyant suffusions of light, of space being exacerbated with a diffusion of often almost imperceptible grains of material, until it turns itself into a state of pearlescence; of learning how to see in a different way, of somehow being encouraged to feel freer and more responsive and responsible.

External Window, 1985
The Pace Gallery, New York

Art-In-Response

Arthur C. Danto

Robert Irwin's *Tilted Planes* (1978) and Richard Serra's *Tilted Arc* (1981) seem a natural pair for forced comparison, not just because the word "tilted" in both titles implies a shared aesthetic, but because both were intended as exemplars of public art. They were public in the specific sense that each defined a public space the primary users of which were not members of the artworld, who would have entered the space in question in order to respond to the work as art, though, given the considerable reputation of each artist, there would doubtless have been pilgrims to either site—had Serra's work not been removed and Irwin's not aborted in the planning stage—whose primary interest would have been in the art, and in particular to the way each work related to its site. *Tilted Arc* and *Tilted Planes*, albeit each in its own markedly different way, referred respectively to Javits Plaza in downtown Manhattan, and to the Oval Mall of Ohio State University in Columbus, Ohio. The primary users of the former space would have been employees and clients of a government building to which the plaza architecturally belonged, and, of the latter, students and teachers entering and leaving the classroom buildings which ringed the space's perimeter, crisscrossing the somewhat eccentric system of paths which connected entryway with entryway. Each space had a secondary use as a recreational area—a welcome outdoor patch for office workers to take their lunch breaks, and a kind of academic grove in which students grouped on lawns in fine weather, or played frisbee, or, in periods of political effervescence, held demonstrations.

The parallels and similarities of the two works do not greatly extend beyond this point, where in fact they begin quite radically to diverge. It will serve the purposes of an essay on Irwin's conception of public art to make these divergences explicit, a strategy which will have the incidental effect of underscoring the heterogeneity of the designation and the meaning of the term "public art." As public artists, Irwin and Serra could not be more different.

In the first place, *Tilted Arc* dominated the space for which it was conceived to the point where it subverted the basic functions of the space, treating it virtually as if its sole role were to be a kind of extended base for Serra's sculpture. Workers and clients were obliged to find their way round the work in order to enter or leave the building; and it partitioned the plaza as effectively as the Wall cut Germany into distinct geographical realities. Never especially hospitable—windy, often wet, shadowed by sullen office structures—Javits Plaza became even less so than it had been before it was invaded by Art. Office-workers, not educated to the aesthetics of rust, nor in the exquisite placement of works of sculpture, found the work ugly, confrontational, domineering, and alien to the fundamental human purposes the space had heretofore served. Inevitably they protested its presence, making way for a contest between art experts on the one side, whose vision of public art was predominately aesthetic and for whom it sufficed that Serra's work had unquestioned artistic merit; and, on the other side, the ordinary men and women who may not have seen eye to eye with the experts on matters of what constitutes art, but who knew they had been deprived of an amenity rendered suddenly poignant by its loss.

By marked contrast with *Tilted Arc*, *Tilted Planes* would have been all but invisible; and indeed, had it been executed as Irwin intended, there would have been nothing separate and identifiable as *Tilted Planes* which could be seen as such. It would have stood to its site in roughly the relationship in which spirit stands to matter or mind to body; and its near-invisibility would be metaphysically of a piece with the invisibility of each of the left-hand members of these pairs. A photograph of the Oval Mall would *ipso facto* have been a photograph of *Tilted Planes*, but there would have been no way in which one could have made a photograph of just *Tilted Planes*, the way one could of *Tilted Arc* by whiting out Javits Plaza. There would have been no difference between figure and ground in Irwin's work, as there is in a photograph which shows *Tilted Arc* with its urban background: in Irwin's work, figure and ground would be *one*. Wittgenstein says, in the *Philosophical Investigations*, that the human body is the best picture there can be of the human mind. In this sense, the Oval Mall would have been the best picture there could have been of *Tilted Planes*. The work would have been everywhere and nowhere. Of course, there would have been some just-discernable differences in the Oval Mall after *Tilted Planes* was made: certain shadows visible from an aerial perspective, and, to someone who walked across the space, a certain felt difference: a certain easy change in gradients, and some gentle drops. But it would have been altogether possible to traverse the space without recognizing that anything had happened, or that one was walking on a work of art. The Dean, who blocked the project with the wholly understandable query "Where's the sculpture?" asked exactly the right question.

Usually, it is logically implied by the concept of sculpture that there is a "where," a space marked for the placement of the sculpture, which itself has fixed boundaries, *dis*placing a portion of the atmosphere. But this is to assimilate the concept of sculpture to the concept of the *statue*—a movable, detachable piece of worked material such as bronze, aluminum, stone, or steel. In the present case, the boundaries of *Tilted Planes* would have been coincident with the boundaries of the site (which invited an image, under the statue-concept of sculpture, of paving the entire space with steel!). But Irwin in fact uses the concept of sculpture in so non- or even in so anti-statuary a sense that in his view, the Oval Mall was *already* a work of sculpture, whatever might have been the fate of *Tilted Planes*. As he explained to Lawrence Weschler,

> To me, it was already a piece of sculpture. It had all the dimensions and all
> the properties of a piece of sculpture: physical divisions, both organic and

geometric, participation of people, the kinetics of movement. It was already operative in that way.[1]

He immediately concedes that "No one but someone like myself who was pre-occupied with it would even recognize that idea. Not too many people pay attention to that sort of thing." So *Tilted Planes* would have involved the transformation of one piece of sculpture into a momentously but hardly noticeably different piece of sculpture.

By Irwin's criterion, Javits Plaza too was already a piece of sculpture, but, clearly, an artist like Richard Serra, with his largely statuary concept of sculpture, would hardly have seen it that way at all. His view of the Plaza was of an aesthetically undistinguished open space, a pure spatial potentiality awaiting artistic actualization through the placement in it of a work of art. The Dean at Ohio State might not have been prepared to accommodate so abstract a presence as *Tilted Arc* to his vision of art, but he hardly could have wondered *where* the sculpture was, supposing it were acknowledged by him as sculpture. This work proclaimed its whereness in its scale, its opacity, its conspicuous having-been-fabricatedness. (After its removal, I once suggested a sort of memorial scar, an arc of bronze set in flush with the pavement to memorialize where it had been, commemorating the battle in which the public reclaimed its aesthetic rights from the experts.) At the time of the controversy, it was often argued that *Tilted Arc* could not be moved, mainly because its identity as a work was co-implicated with its placement: it was repeatedly insisted that the work was *site-specific*. Irwin characterizes *his* work as *site-generated* instead. Since what I regard as Irwin's most interesting and challenging work is site-generated rather than site-specific, it will be of some value to distinguish the different relationships to site these expressions imply. Irwin himself is at some pains to explain them in his extremely helpful text, *Being and Circumstance*, but it is worth going over this not altogether familiar ground once again, all the more so in that the dominant impulse of his oeuvre since 1977 is site-generation.

The site-specific work refers to and defines the space into which it is set; and part of its meaning must be specified with regard to these relationships, formal and at times semantical. Thus the curve of *Tilted Arc* may be said in some way to emblematize the shape of the general space for which it was designed; and the assumption is that a quite different work might have been designed had that space been different. Its site-specificity means in effect that the work together with the site form a kind of aesthetic whole: the site is emblematically present in the work, which in turn is a kind of icon for the space to which it inherently belongs. There is certainly a strong distinction between work so conceived and the kind of public art exemplified by what is sometimes disparaged as the "corporate bauble"—a Henry Moore statue placed in front of corporate headquarters, say, proclaiming the commitment to artistic values of the highest sort on the part of the corporation, which enhances its image by association with the recognizable style of a renowned master. Budgets may not always allow, of course, for the purchase or commission of a Moore— or a Calder or a Smith— but then the kind of art displayed will in any case transmit, in the rhetoric of cultural signs, the kinds of values with which the corporation means to identify itself. These works can, often in consequence of their value, be transferred to museums without losing much if anything of their meaning: Michelangelo's *David*, Rodin's *Balzac*, are cases in point, in which an ornamental and symbolic function was overridden by the artistic value of the works, which finally transcended their original sites. They were promoted to the inventory of the world's works of art, and placed in protective custody.

In large measure, the same could have happened with *Tilted Arc*. Space was set aside for it, for example, in the Storm King sculpture garden, north of New York, where it might have led a life of pure aesthetic placement forever. Serra resisted this, perhaps rightly, on the grounds that the work was specific to the site and had no identity apart from it, and he clearly had the courage of his convictions: the work now sits disassembled in storage, perhaps awaiting a Napoleonic return. Now without question there may have been features of the site without reference to which the work could not have been appreciated in its full meaning. But there are a good many steel arcs by Serra which are every bit as freestanding as the *David*. The work does not wear, so to speak, its site-specificity on its sleeve. And it is not difficult to argue that the main relationship between the steel arc and its place is very largely external and designatory: its "meaning," that is, does not penetrate its form to any significant extent. And the mere fact that it should have occurred naturally to the directors of Storm King that the work could be translocated there is evidence that even in the curatorial mind the work is perceived as having an independent and detachable being. A sign, say a sign which consists in an arrow, is clearly site-specific, in that if it is removed from that to which it was constructed to point, its meaning will have been lost: it becomes an abstract deictic shape. Still, someone could place it in The Museum of Signs. It exists as an object. Even in its present dismantled state *Tilted Arc* remains an object—so many units of Cor-Ten steel, weighing so much and having thus and such dimensions.

Nothing remotely like this could have been true of *Tilted Planes*. Its being is so indissolubly mingled with the being of its site that it can have no detached and separate existence. It is, as the philosopher Bishop Berkeley once said in regard to minds or spirits, incapable of being an object. Had it been realized as a work and afterward objected to for whatever reason to the point where its removal was mandated, there would really be nothing left over when it was taken away. Or nothing for which a separate site, like that at Storm King, could be imagined. It would revert to mere materials—some truckloads of dirt and a few retaining walls of Cor-Ten steel. And to its previous status as a plan, a project, an idea—which is its present state of being. Its being is merely on paper now, but even had it achieved what philosophers once called "formal reality," in space and time and external to its various representations in the mind of the artist or in his drawings, it would not have existed as a separable

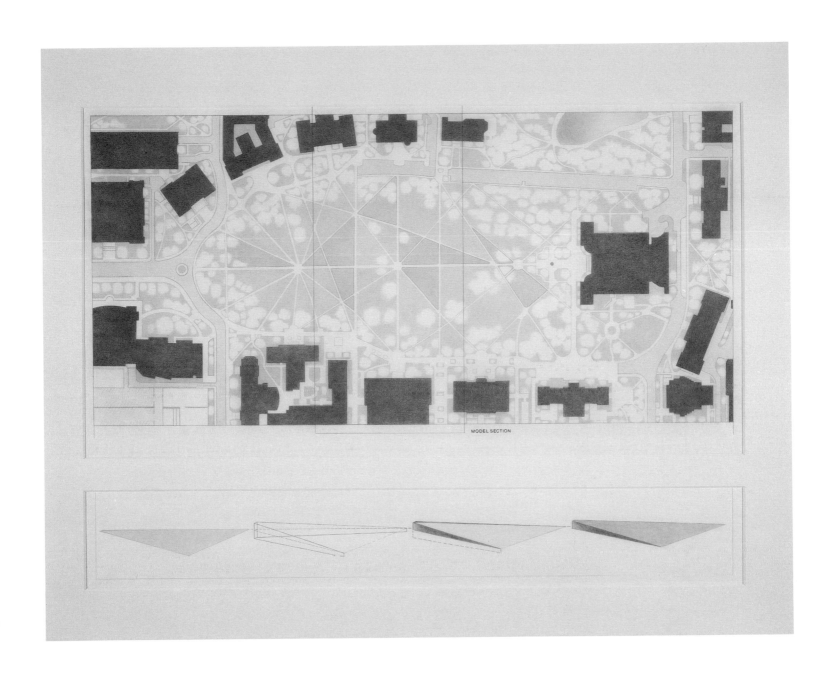

MODEL SECTION

Tilted Planes, proposed 1978
Oval Mall, Ohio State University,
Columbus
Project drawing

object. It is precisely non-objective art in the meaning of that term which I hope is now quite clear: it is art that has no separate material existence as an object.

We are now, I think, in position to say what it was in that site which "generated" *Tilted Planes*, and what in general are the salient features of non-objective site-generated art as practiced, perhaps uniquely, by Robert Irwin. *Tilted Planes* was among the earliest of Irwin's exercises in what he terms "art-in-response," which means that in contrast with the kind of artist who creates, so to speak, out of his or her own substance a body of works done "on spec," which are then shown, bought, sold, collected, exchanged, Irwin generates art only in response to the invitation to do so, and then in specific response to whatever it was that occasioned the invitation. "I am no longer concerned with the art world context," he confessed to Weschler in 1979. "I'll use any materials, any techniques (I don't care if somebody else is using them or seems to have them earmarked; I don't care if they're thought of as art or non-art), *anything that references against the specific conditions of the site.* Whether it works is my only criterion."[2] No one can really know whether or not *Tilted Planes* works, of course, but Irwin has said on more than one occasion that it is among his most successful pieces to date, which I take as my justification for so protracted a discussion of it as a paradigm of his artistic agenda. As with so many of his projects, this was part of a competition, in this instance sponsored by the University Art Gallery of Ohio State. Strikingly, Richard Serra was in the initial roster of those invited to compete, and though every creative artist is creative in his or her own way, it is not unreasonable to surmise what sort of work he would have submitted. Irwin's proposal was by contrast entirely unpredictable. He approaches a site with nothing specific in mind by way of the art he will propose, letting the work, whatever it is to be, emerge out of the objective conditions of the site as he perceives them. Serra at that time was placing monumental steel sculptures at various sites; Tony Smith—another artist on the short list—would have been placing his signature black metal pieces. These would be identifiably sculptures in readily identified styles. Irwin, in that sense, has no style, only a philosophy of openness and response, and in truth his proposal on this occasion resembles nothing that had been done before. *Tilted Planes* emerges from his acknowledgment that the Oval Mall was the symbolic and in certain ways the functional center of the institution. His project was finally a response to the question of how to transform into considered art what made the Oval Mall the crucial indispensable site it was.

This meant a kind of underlining of its most palpable features, which were the various paths which crossed and recrossed the space in a not quite regular pattern of diagonals. The irregularity was due to the fact that the lines reflected paths spontaneously taken by students heading from one building to another, which then were paved after the pattern had been established. It is a kind of monument to the natural bent of a given society to trace the patterns of its being onto the surface of the world: a sort of natural script. This characterization, however, treats the paths as figure to the Oval's ground: the grass intersected by the paths is almost read as a blank sheet

Tilted Planes
Project model

on which the script unfurled itself. What Irwin did was to reverse the figure-ground relationship, emphasizing the paths by emphasizing the spaces between the paths, which became the "planes" of the title. He did this by literally tilting some of them, transforming them, as it were, into grassed facets of a figure which seemed to conform to a certain fractal formula. The Oval became a sort of three-dimensional entity, and the planes mark the edges and vertices of the now salient planes.

Not all the planes tilt, but the somewhat subliminal difference between those that do and those that don't immediately defines the two distinct kinds of areas which at present intermingle: areas where students engage in strenuous campus recreations (like frisbee throwing); and those where groups sit on the lawns to discuss things, or individuals study out of doors. This quite geometrical division of function— so different, after all, from planting signs which interdict certain activities and so encourage the possibility of resistance to authority, is typical of Irwin's solution to human problems. He is an astute psychologist, and the shapes of his designs reflect, or at least take into consideration, the ways in which the minds of users will characteristically respond: the more strenuous activities find, as it were, their natural sites on the flat planes. But the gradients are sufficiently gentle not to discourage sitting in circles. A further and ingenious feature of the *Tilted Planes* is that the edges which are at the highest points above the paths—from eighteen inches to perhaps thirty inches —constitute what one might designate "natural benches": comfortable, grass-upholstered ledges where pedestrians can sit and let their legs dangle. The edges themselves are neatly formed by bands of Cor-Ten which, with their natural rusting surfaces, look like sod. So the planes turn insidiously into benches without the need for what Irwin calls "the addition of cumbersome street furniture."[3] Perhaps a word of criticism might be ventured at this point. One cannot help but wonder to what degree the idea of a grassy natural bench is not an expression of a climactic Southern California optimism, or perhaps of the artist having been somewhat taken in by the idyllic images of students lounging on lawns, beneath the trees, which universities use in their publicity to encourage a certain arcadian vision. Midwestern winters would tend to make "natural furniture" unusable through the many months of the year when "street furniture" would still make possible the taking of the sun of a winter afternoon without getting one's bottom soaked through!

Be this as it may, *Tilted Planes* can hardly be bettered as a teaching example for Irwin's aesthetic and his methodology as public artist. His best response-driven work will be site-generated; will be non-objective; and will use the natural psychological dispositions of users of the site to provide the ideal amenities of which the site is capable. And of course the work will be unforeseeable: it will require the actual response of the artist to the actual site, at which his intuitions as to what the site "wants" will be mobilized. There is a certain conceptual precedent for this, perhaps, in Michelangelo's famous idea that as a sculptor he sought to discover, literally uncover, the figure already present in the stone, so that sculpting for him, at least as he saw it, was a procedure for removing matter from form, liberating the figure from the imprisoning stone. Michelangelo would certainly not have thought of himself as imposing his will-to-form on passive matter. Nor does Irwin think this way either. His task as an artist is to give the site, understood essentially in human terms, what the site "wants" for itself in terms of how it is to be used and what its meaning is to be relative to that use. He has often said, in my presence, that there may very well be occasions on which the cannon-on-the lawn is the ideal solution to the kind of problem which defines his art, and it might be worth dwelling on this radical and surprising formulation for what it tells us about the way he thinks as an artist.

The cannon-on-the-lawn formulation tells us at the very least that we are not to thematize the tilted triangles and polygons of *Tilted Planes* as evidence of a certain resolute drop-dead Minimalism on the artist's part. It is true that his early work bounded on Minimalism, though its motivations were almost always different from those which drove the official Minimalists of the East Coast. It just happened that the ideal solution for *this* problem called for geometrical shapes. But Irwin was no more wedded to the rhetoric of geometry than he was to certain materials which had become virtual signature materials for him: scrim, for notable example, or glass or plastic. The materials for *Tilted Planes* are enumerated as "Cor-Ten steel, concrete footings, and re-sod grass." He had already used floral motifs in his work which the more doctrinaire Minimalist would have impugned as "decorative." Such motifs suggested themselves naturally in his 1979 *Filigreed Line* project for Wellesley College, and somewhat less naturally in the *Two Ceremonial Gates, Asian Pacific Basin* (1983) designed for the San Francisco International Airport. He there employs without embarrassment what look like wisteria blossoms alongside a flowing stream. He really meant it when he emphasized his readiness to "use anything that references against the specific conditions of the site." So why not a cannon, if that should "reference" against the specific conditions of a site? You cannot tell in advance of the invitation what may be called for.

As a philosopher of art, I have often used examples which consist of pairs of objects which are all but indiscernible—which look more or less alike—but where one is a work of art and the other not. My best case was the *Brillo Box* by Andy Warhol, a 1964 sculpture whose photograph would look indistinguishable from the ordinary corrugated cartons in which Brillo pads were routinely packed, and to be found in the storerooms of supermarkets. My strategy was in part to emphasize that you cannot define visual art in visual terms alone, since no interesting visual differences exist between *Brillo Box* (for example) and the Brillo boxes. Or, if there are differences, surely the distinction between art and reality hardly can be accounted for in terms of them! The artworld has been exceedingly fertile in such examples: there is no interesting visual difference between the photograph of a sharecropper woman by Walker Evans and its rephotographing by Sherrie Levine. Both, to be sure, are works of art, but they have deeply different meanings and certainly different semantics. Evans's is of a person, Levine's is of a photograph, and a very famous one at that. The difference is less to do with looking but with knowing what the history and theory of the two images is. After all, the differences between the Oval Mall before and after *Tilted Planes* is minimal and yet in some ways monumental. The patterns would be indiscernible, but the meanings would diverge greatly, in part because *Tilted Planes* would be about the Oval Mall.

So it would be an interesting exercise to try to imagine a site Irwin would respond to by the placement of a cannon and, let us suppose, a neat pile of cannon balls, in contrast with the rather banal sites with cannons and piled cannon balls found in hamlets and villages throughout the nation, from wherever men went off to fight in wars. Our imagined site would resemble these to whatever degree one wishes, and the differences need not be visual at all. It is not for me to construct the scenario in which Irwin's generated response to a site would consist in the cannon. But cannons are symbols drenched in certain generic meanings, of memorialization, of stifled violence, of military narrative, or young persons lost, of the rhetoric of military glory and defeat. The very presence of cannons must activate a cluster of associations. A critic seeing such a work might correctly and at the same time irrelevantly say that "it had all been done before." It would be essential to its meaning that it had been done before. But it would equally be essential to its meaning that it had not been done before at all, for those other cannons would not have been placed there because "it had all been done before!" This cannon would be site-generated, and perhaps make reference to all those sites. I can even imagine Irwin designing a cannon and having it fabricated to his specifications. Some of his works look as though they incorporate elements which had been salvaged, or found in junkyards, when in truth Irwin designed them, did the drawings, and oversaw their fabrication. He just happened to need something that looked as if it belonged to an earlier era.

Filigreed Line, 1980
Wellesley College,
Massachusetts

Sponsored by Jewett Arts Center,
Wellesley College

3/8-inch stainless steel, pattern
plasma cut; concrete footings

A low-profile line of stainless steel runs along
the top of a rolling plane of grass. The leaflike
cutouts echo the patterns of the trees.

Nine Spaces, Nine Trees, 1983
Public Safety Building Plaza,
Seattle

Sponsored by the City of Seattle,
the Seattle Arts Commission,
and the National Endowment
for the Arts

Cast concrete planters; Kolorgaard
5/8-inch aperture, plastic-coated
blue fencing; Visuvius plum trees
and *sedum oreganium* ground cover

The plan for this project was keyed by nine
columns (loading points) in the police garage
below the plaza. An architecture of nine spaces
is drawn in blue fencing material around the
flowering violet plum trees centering each space.

A Single Plane: 324 Parts, 1985
San Francisco Museum
of Modern Art

360 blocks, 2 x 2 x 4 feet each,
16 wall steel box tubes 1 by 1
by 10 feet 6 1/2 inches each,
voile tergal (scrim)

In the rotunda of the museum, nine sections of
thirty-six two-by-two-by-four-feet boxes form a
single white plane mirroring the skylight above.

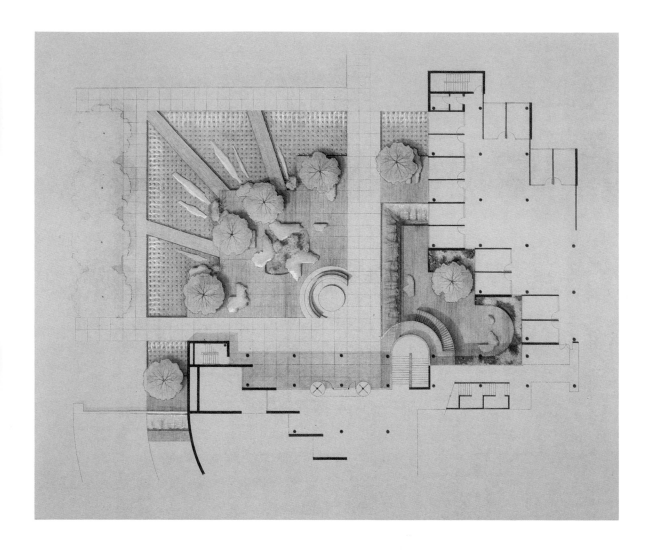

H.H.H. Memorial Plaza,
proposed 1983 (unrealized)
Hubert Horatio Humphrey Center
University of Minnesota,
Minneapolis

Sponsored by the Center for
Art and the Environment

Granite, steel grating, concrete,
water, plantings

At the entrance to the H.H.H. Center, a plaza
of open stainless steel decking, interspersed
with Russian olive trees and large granite rock
seating, floats over a flow of white water.

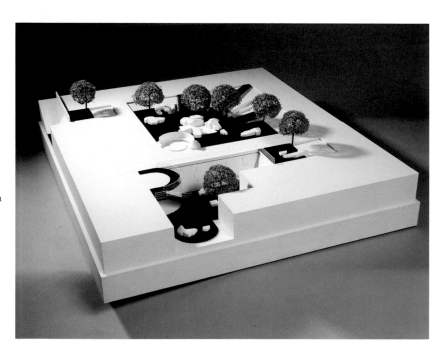

142

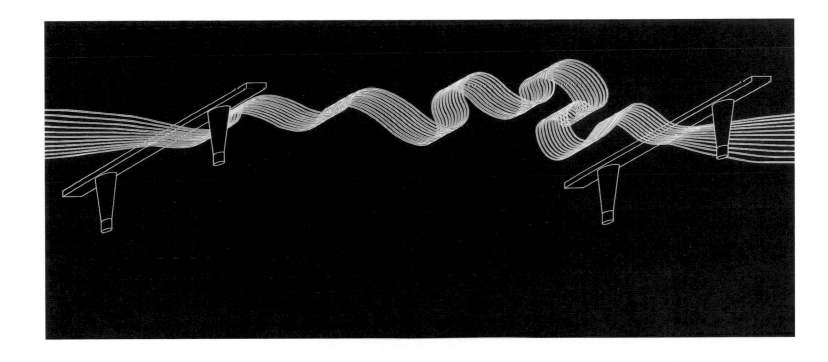

Grand Avenue Viaduct,

proposed 1985 (unrealized)
Upper and lower Grand Avenues,
Los Angeles

Sponsored by Bunker Hill
Associates and The Museum of
Contemporary Art, Los Angeles

Specially-designed extruded
aluminum fluorescent fixtures
(lower Grand Avenue), stainless
steel fluorescent fixtures (upper
Grand Avenue)

Eleven lines of blue-white fluorescent light —
corresponding to eleven structural beams —
begin at the end walls of lower Grand Avenue,
proceed up to the lower level ceiling, collect
together, then swing upward through the open-
ings to appear on upper Grand Avenue as two
fluid configurations of flowing planes of light.

143

The federal eagle, done in a sort of Art Deco manner, which is a component of *Sentinel Plaza* in Pasadena, California, is a case in point. It is archly styled, faces in the four directions of a compass as a sentinel eagle should, and its wings are drawn up like the closed petals of a lotus flower, but poised for flight. It surmounts a column of cast granite, and is in turn surmounted by a blue-violet lamp which proclaims the identity of the building behind it as in fact a police station. The whole lamp—ornament, column, light—has the air of having been rescued from a site from the WPA years. It and the whole remainder of *Sentinel Plaza* have a kind of cannon-on-the-lawn dimension: the piece looks as though at least parts of it had been there for centuries. There is, for example, a sort of basin with a trough, made of fitted stones and planted about with echevaria— drought-tolerant succulents which emphasize the thin course of water which runs along the trough. In style, it fits the postmodern police building designed by Robert Stern, heavy as it is with Spanish Colonial Baroque references, such as the heavy volutes above the portico. The basin-with-trough in fact is a kind of fountain, the thin stream of which celebrates the preciousness of water (by contrast with the boisterous fountains of Rome, which celebrate water's plenitude). The desert plants convey the same message. And so does the double-trunked sycamore

Sentinel Plaza, 1990
Pasadena Police Department

tree, by Irwin's reckoning the centerpiece of the work and its most expensive single component. The sycamore too has the appearance of having stood there for centuries, casting its sparse shadow over the place, and indeed nothing visual will mark the difference between the tree-as-art and a mere tree which is merely a tree. In fact the sycamore belongs to a system of symbols already, which is why Irwin chose it. It connotes water: the Indians used to make their kayaks from the trunk. It binds everything in the plaza—the fountain, the plantings, even the riverbed gravel which composes the surface—into a complex of meanings. There is behind this complex a painted wall which has begun to undergo a beautiful patination, insinuating use and wear and age. Someone, hearing that Irwin had executed a commission in Pasadena might, knowing that he once did Minimalist paintings, see the wall as the art, so compelling is the domination by painting of our concept of art. But in fact the wall is no more the art than the tree is or the gravel. The art is one with the place. Work and site are seamlessly a unity.

Close of kin with *Sentinel Plaza* is the unexecuted City Front Plaza, which was to have been in downtown Chicago, in front of the insurance company which com-

missioned it but filed for bankruptcy before work could begin. It would precisely have illustrated the cannon-on-the-lawn principle, inasmuch as there would have been nothing especially contemporary about the two sixty-foot towers in which the site was principally to have consisted. One of them, indeed, looks as though it might have antedated the Eiffel Tower in its ornamental cast-iron verticality and airy elegance. The drawings for this tower look as though they might have been executed by a nineteenth-century draughtsman. One might think Irwin would sell these drawings, somewhat in the manner in which Christo markets drawings and prints to finance his various projects.

Irwin refers to these somewhat disparagingly as postcards, but his refusal to treat his own drawings as art in their own right goes some distance toward marking the internal difference between public art as he conceives of it, and as Christo does, though there are certainly outward similarities between the two artists. For Christo, the political processes leading up to the execution of the work are, however frustrating, as important as the work, in that the entire community will have been brought into the discussion. For Irwin, all this is external, a matter of obstacles to be gotten round, and often destructive of the work: he told me that of the twenty-five competitions he had won, only one actually achieved completion. And for each of the twenty-four unfulfilled projects, there is a tale of politics, resistance, bureaucracy, suspicion, or, as with the tower complex for Chicago, sheer bad luck: a company fails, a patron dies, the person in authority retires. Christo, again in contrast with Irwin, very much imposes his artistic will onto a preexisting site, skirting islands with pink plastic, dotting a landscape with umbrellas, wrapping structures in plastic, piling oildrums up in the shape of a *mastaba*. His work is site-dominant, to use Irwin's vocabulary, rather than site-generated. And because of the notoriety of certain of his works, Christo will often be invited to "wrap something," which a community may perceive as an event with a certain newsworthiness and visibility. Christo interacts with the community, there is an active dialogue, whereas Irwin, while not opposed to education, tries to enlist the psychology of users to achieve the goals of a work, as with the differential gradients of *Tilted Planes*. And then Irwin pretty much depends upon his inviters to find the money, whereas Christo makes a point of his work costing the community nothing, covering his own expenses with the sale of drawings, film rights, publications, and the like. But Irwin's non-objective conception of art rules out selling what social critics sometimes speak of as commodified art. I don't think Irwin is

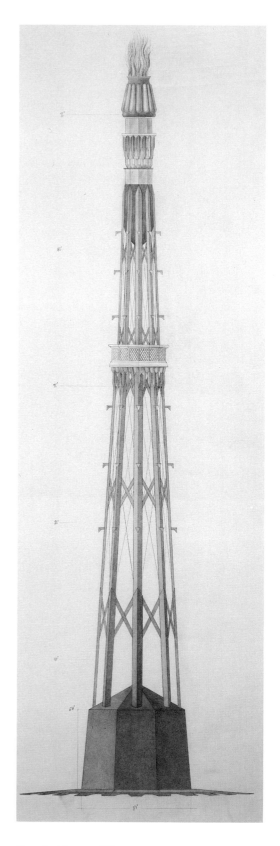

Two Architectural Towers,
proposed 1989 (unrealized)
City Front Plaza, Chicago

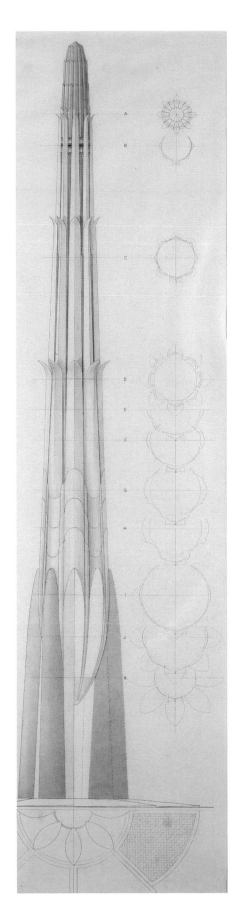

especially ideological on this point, but merely consistent with his agenda. So, marvelous as the drawings are, even to the point of exquisiteness, it would be a subversion of their function to treat them as objects-of-art: that is not the way an artist-in-response *works*.

The two towers refer to the surrounding towers of downtown Chicago, to which landscape, of course, they belong. But their reference is far wider than that. Tower One refers to the industrial history of Chicago, set as it is on a base in the form of a gear, soaring upward in a surge of rotarian confidence to where a flame is lit, of the sort one sees in oil refineries burning off impurities, and serving here as a flambeau of progress. There was to have been a concealed tank so that water could mist down which would, in winter, freeze along the internal cables. The iced-iron filigree would have been underlit by a blue spot in the base. And the complex symbolism of industry and progress would be fused with an Aristotelian symbolism of fire and water. That would leave the elements of earth and air in Tower Two, which, in Irwin's description, is "a stalk-like aluminum shaft that turns into a faceted glass top light." In fact, Tower Two has a certain affinity with the quadruple eagle of *Sentinel Plaza*, inasmuch as it looks like a poised rocket as conceived of by a thirties designer, someone influenced, say, by Raymond Loewy. The rocket form inevitably unites earth and air, poised as it is for flight.

Had the two towers been erected, it is difficult to believe, for all that they refer and emblematize their towered ambience, that they could be considered altogether non-objective. One could imagine a time when they might have been removed to some museum-like site, to be sure at a certain loss of meaning, given that the drama of their presence is underwritten by their intended original location. But that danger would not be faced by Irwin's proposal for the expansion of Miami International Airport, which is immeasurably more complex than *Tilted Planes*, but which would have been—which is, as concept—no less successful than it. I think it fair to designate the Miami Airport Project Irwin's masterpiece. He put several years into developing it and learned a lot from the process. Had the project gone through it would almost certainly have revolutionized airport design. Miami International Airport would have been a brilliant fusion of function and amenity which would, at the same time, hardly have been noticed as such by its users, even though nearly every move they made in approaching, in waiting, and in leaving the airport would have been subtly directed in Irwin's astonishingly detailed plan. I shall conclude this essay by discussing this extraordinary conception, in which all the components of Irwin's artistic philosophy are brought together and raised to their highest level to date.

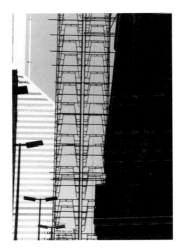

Source material for
Two Architectural Towers

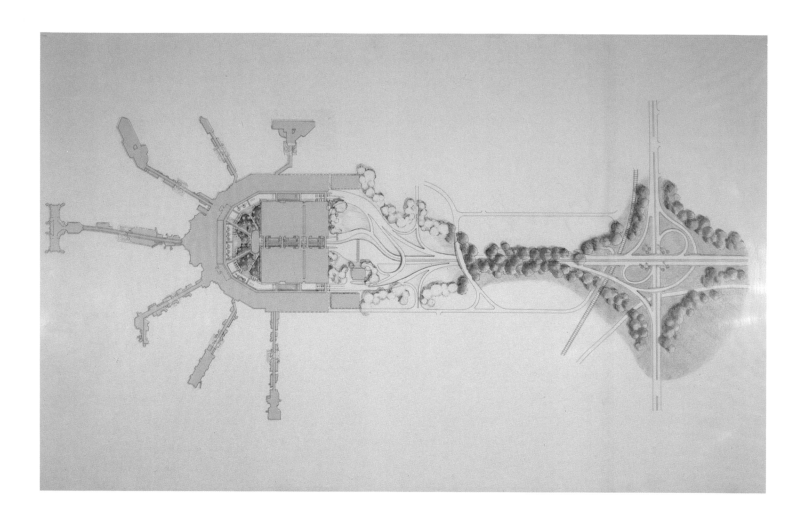

Irwin's approach to the airport was characteristically novel, but it was in fact more deeply novel than could be inferred on the basis of his previous response-oriented art, although the Miami project carries over into the new schematism a great many of the values and strategies inherent in its predecessors. It has become commonplace for airports, like any number of public agencies, to commission a piece of art, but usually this will be by way of adjunction: an artwork is adjoined to an existing complex, and serves as an ornament which does not penetrate the larger meaning of the site. To be sure, artists may make the effort to represent the function of the place in one or another way. The Miami airport had at one point a mural by James Rosenquist, which had an oblique reference to flight in its iconography. But for the most part, airport public art is typically of the bauble category, a spot of aesthetic afterthought calculated to grace a site whose essential business of moving people off the ground into the air and vice versa goes on perfectly adequately without benefit of the art. Needless to say, this would never have been Irwin's way if he could help it, and he basically reinvented the relationship in which art and the airport experience were to stand to one another. It is a tribute to his considerable powers of persuasion that he actually convinced the airport administration of the viability, indeed of the necessity of this radical arrangement.

Arts Enrichment Master Plan,
proposed 1986 (unrealized)
Miami International Airport,
Miami, Florida
Drawing

Of course, one could not begin completely from scratch; Miami's was a preexisting structure. Even so, Irwin's idea was that he should participate fully in the planning of the airport, that there should at every stage be decisions in which the input of artists would materially enhance the final result. Irwin devoted himself to establishing the relationship between art and design engineering at crucial points in the passengers' movement through the airport. His project assumes that the airport, the first and last part of the city a traveler experiences, should in some way emblematize the city, rather than serve some impersonal outskirt function, architecturally everywhere and nowhere. This involved him in the design of approach roads, parking, rental car return sites, and of the roads back to the metropolitan center. What is emblematic of Miami is the abundance of water (as water is emblematic of Pasadena by its scarcity). The road from airport to city and back again should traverse typical Dade County waterscape, planted with palmettos and reeds. But there should be no scenic distraction at the point of approach where drivers must find their way to departure, arrival, and parking sites. Irwin designed a cool corridor through which one headed to these various destinations, and the pattern of the driver's experience was an alternation of shade and light. And he designed a marvelous "central park," filled with plant and even bird life, an amenity for spiritual restoration as needed by travelers, leave-takers, greeters. Artists would enhance the way windows worked, and would collaborate on the placement of Florida-like installations in the various approaches to the gates. In the end, the entire airport would be art, and, of course, it would at the same time be nothing but what it is, a busy international gateway, the users of which need hardly be mindful of the marvelous way art has been used to ease their passage. One of the goals of art in such projects is, Irwin states in a sort of flowchart, to "heighten awareness." Not to heighten awareness of art as art, but of the dimensions and features of life that art raises to the highest powers of enhancement while remaining invisible, directing the viewer's sensibilities with a kind of aesthetic Hidden Hand.

The great Constructivist visionary, Alexander Rodchenko, invented the slogan "Art into Life!". He meant that artists were not to make the traditional sorts of things—paintings and sculptures—that hang in frames or stand on pedestals in prosperous salons. Characteristically, he and his followers transformed objects of use with fine bold designs: clothing, book covers, stage sets, posters. Irwin has, as with *Tilted Planes*, added a third dimension to this formulation. Anything can be art without having to look like art at all. The task he has set himself, as he says explicitly in the epilogue of his text *Being and Circumstance*, is "to enable us to experience beauty in everything." Art is the means to that rather than its object.

Notes

1. Lawrence Weschler, *Seeing is Forgetting the Name of the Thing One Sees: A Life of Contemporary Artist Robert Irwin* (Berkeley and Los Angeles: University of California Press, 1982), pp.198-99.

2. Ibid., p.193.

3. Robert Irwin, *Being and Circumstance: Notes Toward a Conditional Art* (Larkspur Landing, Calif.: The Lapis Press, 1985), p.43.

Playing It As It Lays & Keeping It In Play:

A Visit with Robert Irwin

Lawrence Weschler

The entire enterprise—a Robert Irwin *retrospective*, that retrospective's *catalogue*, an *essay* for that catalogue—veritably basks in contradiction.

With Irwin, after all, we are dealing with an artist whose work's very essence is experience—how it presents itself at the moment it is being experienced—and yet most of that work, certainly the work of the last two decades, isn't really there to be experienced, either because it no longer exists (it was only intended to last a week or a month), or because it never existed (it never even got built), or because even though it does exist, it cannot be transported from place to place so as to be *re*experienced. It can't be transported from place to place because—perhaps more so than with the work of any other artist—it simply *is* the place it has endeavored to attend.

Photographs exist—diagrams, blueprints, models. But in a profound sense these have nothing whatsoever to do with the work. For a long time Irwin even forbade the photographing of his work—and this was when he was still making the sorts of objects (paintings, discs, columns) which might arguably have been photographed. An early intuition in this regard hardened into absolute conviction: photographs, he felt, would inevitably capture none of what the work was about and everything that it was not. Photos, that is, could at best convey the work's image but never its presence. And presence—immediate, phenomenal experience; not a metaphor for presence but presence itself—has with ever increasing urgency been the principal focus of Irwin's concern.

Words exist—anecdotes, analyses, recapitulations—and indeed it is one of the many paradoxes surrounding this particular master of the ineffable that he himself is immensely loquacious, garrulous, expansively opinionated, at times even prolix. His written voice can be as dense, clotted, and difficult as his spoken voice is breezy, easy, and spry. But the point is that the work is all about the sort of attention that *precedes* verbalization, about what it's like to experience—or rather, what it *is* to experience—before being overwhelmed by words. This is why I entitled my 1982 biography of Irwin, adapting a line of Paul Valéry's, *Seeing is Forgetting the Name of the Thing One Sees*: in part because that kind of struck-dumb attentiveness was precisely the sort of experience to which Irwin's works were increasingly aspiring, but also because my text constituted a record of all the things, the usual taken-for-granted components of the art act—image, line, focus, frame, signature, naming, the requirement of making itself—which Irwin himself had had sequentially to jettison, to bracket out, *to forget*, before he himself was able to see. Being here now is what Irwin is all about—*getting* here now—not talking about it. And yet "getting it" breeds talk—his, ours—and there is in Irwin's work all sorts of stuff to talk about.

As I say, the entire enterprise basks in contradiction.

Irwin himself is one of the most interestingly and fruitfully contradictory figures on the art scene today, as I recalled recently when I flew out to San Diego to visit him. Which is to say, he's hardly changed at all. Los Angeles has changed, or so he was telling me as we eased out of the airport parking lot in his 1982 Cadillac Eldorado, a sleek black boat of a car (ten years ago, in L.A., he'd been driving a ten-year-old *silver* Eldorado). The freeways are perpetually clogged, which eliminates one of the chief attractions the place used to hold for him. He basically left L.A. about ten years ago, in part to get away from the traffic and in part to get away from the jabber of the art scene, settling first in Las Vegas, where he lived in a glass-walled apartment, near the top of the city's tallest apartment building. (Back in New York during those days, I used to look at my watch whenever the sun was setting, and three hours later I'd telephone Bob to hear the latest on his wrastlings with Kant and Wittgenstein—he was mainly reading during that period—and, in passing, to get his spectacularly vivid running account of the sun's setting over the desert there.) "One of the nice things about San Diego," he was telling me now, as we suddenly veered into the parking lot of a Winchell's donut stand—"Just a second, right back." He hopped out of the car, dove into the stand, and reemerged a few seconds later, bearing two cups of Coke, one of which he handed me. Bob's never really at home in any new city till he's tracked down the place with the perfectly calibrated Cokes—it usually takes several months of assiduous field research. "As you can see," he joked, "I've located my source." He restarted the car, and his point: "One of the nice things about San Diego," he said, "is that I've managed to find a neighborhood that's an awful lot like L.A. in the fifties. Very laid back and stable. Half the residents went to high school right there. There's no gentrification, which is only because nobody's selling: there's a lot of pressure to sell, a lot to be gained monetarily in selling, but who'd want to leave? A lot of my neighbors work nearby, in the sailmaking shops and other small businesses nestled along the water. As you can see"—we were approaching it now, the Point Loma district straddling the hills overlooking the northern mouth of San Diego Bay—"real nice in-and-out. You can wake up in the morning, walk out on the deck and see what kind of day it's going to be. It could easily make you happy if you didn't watch yourself." He laughed his characteristic laugh (I've often thought that if they ever made a movie of Irwin's life—not a bad idea—the breezy, flinty James Garner, circa his *Rockford* era, would make a damn close approximation).

He pulled the Eldorado into a small underground parking garage. We got out and took the elevator up to the apartment building's third (and top) floor and then walked along an airy exterior balustrade to the apartment he shares with Adele, his wife of four years (she was away that week, visiting relatives back east). A profusion of exotic, thriving cacti and succulents crowded the welcome mat outside his front door. The apartment itself was bright, white, wonderfully airy, with wide bay windows facing the wide bay, mirrors multiplying the wide bay view, unexpected skylights pouring forth their own airy spray of sky. The sliding glass door, opening out onto a narrow balcony, looked as if it were permanently open (more cacti spread across the balcony deck). There was, as before, as elsewhere, no art on the walls—not Irwin's and not anybody else's. There were, as before, several Plexiglas vitrines containing an astonishing array of mounted, splayed butterflies in an almost delirious variety of hues and patterns. But the main impression was of the bay, the great wide bowl of light. "There's a real magical quality to this bay," Irwin was now telling me—in the distance, on the water's far shore, the skyscrapers of downtown San Diego glistened in the afternoon sun, and beyond them loomed the low brown mountains of Mexico. "And the main feature about it is its absolute silence. This is a terrifically busy harbor, the Navy has the place churning all the time. I can sit here and watch the fleet coming in and going out at all hours of the day. Sometimes one of the big carriers will float in—so big, so close, you feel like you could just lean out and touch it. It seems to take up the entire visual field. *And not a sound.* Absolute silence. I don't know why —maybe it has to do with the surrounding topography, the baffle of the hills—but it's as if the bay just swallowed up all the noise." A flock of pelicans floated by in the mid distance; closer in, a hummingbird darted and froze before the feeder dangling from the balcony's rafters.

Robert and Adele Irwin

As usual, Irwin's wide, slightly angled drafting table faced the view, and, as usual, it was teeming with drawings for new projects. In particular that day he was working on a proposal for a roundabout in a new residential subdivision outside Las Vegas. Basically he was proposing a gently sloping mound, and for on top of the mound—"Look at this here," he said. He pulled out some large blown-up photographs of a desolate desert hillscape. "I was taking a walk a few weeks ago in the desert," Irwin explained, "and I began climbing this hill, and suddenly there these things were—look at them—an entire ridge, hundreds of yards, of these towering reddish-black monoliths, wedged, jammed one up against the other, like a procession of elders, like Stonehenge, like Easter Island. Incredible things: look at the subtle gradations of color. It turned out that they were all part of a quarry. I came down the hill, tracked the quarry guy down, and made a deal: tied up the entire ridge. I'm not sure what I'm going to do with them, but I've been eyeing this mound in Las Vegas."

Stacked about his drafting table on the floor were books on desert rocks and samples of desert rocks as well. Reference works on plants (everything from xeriscape to bougainvillea) were piled atop manuals on civil engineering. Underneath the table behind him, he'd stashed a trove of drawing tubes, vaguely sorted by project. Large zippered folios and Fed-Exed manila envelopes leaned

South Roundabout,

proposed 1992
Las Vegas

Sponsored by the Las Vegas
Arts Commission and
Howard Hughes Corporation

Plant material, rocks

Set on a high alluvial plain west of Las Vegas, a
large configuration of black rocks found in the
surrounding desert will stand like a group of old
men, creating a "power spot" which centers a
vehicular roundabout.

against the wall, along with a bolt of diaphanous white scrim material and a rolled swath of narrow-gauge lavender chainlink fencing.

Our conversation ranged easily from one recent or forthcoming project to the next (Pasadena, Pace, Getty, the French Alps . . .), but the project he kept returning to, and the one whose drawings and tubes and models in fact seemed to comprise the plurality of items in his pile, was the Miami Airport.

"That one started the way most of them do," Irwin recalled, as he went over to the pile, pulling out a few of the tubes and starting to unfurl the scrolls inside. "They'd gotten themselves into a jam, and now they were calling out for help. It was another one of those one-percent-for-art type situations that seem to constitute the basis for most of the public art that gets done nowadays. There's a law or a regulation or something requiring that one percent of any big civic construction project's funding be set aside for this amenity called art, there's maybe a municipal or state arts commission that's involved in trying to allocate those funds, invariably it all happens fairly late in the game when most of the construction and design decisions have already been made, and usually they just want some statue or monolith or something they can jam into the middle of the place so that they can say, there, they've done it, they've made the requisite bow to culture. In fact in this case they already had their object—a huge James Rosenquist called *Star Thief* [1980] or something. And everything was going along just fine until Frank Borman, the ex-astronaut, who was heading Eastern Airlines at the time—this was all a few years back when Eastern Airlines still existed and Miami was one of their hubs, they were key customers—anyway, Borman saw this mural and proclaimed, 'I never saw any slab of bacon flying around

in outer space,' and that nixed that. The thing collapsed, and now they were back to starters.

"The city arts commission at the time was headed by an interesting lady named Patricia Fuller, and she saw this as an occasion for a dialogue; so she sent me an invitation. Now, as you know, I get a lot of invitations these days. I get them all the time, and there's generally something a little forlorn about them, because usually the project ends up consuming a lot of time and work and then falling through for one reason or another. But still, it's what I do. I'm like a fire horse. The bell rings and I'm off to the races, the bit chomping in my teeth.

"And this was an interesting situation. I went and looked it over, and afterwards I kept on thinking about it. The airport *was* chaotic, incredibly chaotic. One thing it sure as hell didn't need was more clutter—another object: art. What it was crying out for, though, was an overall approach. And in fact it seemed a perfect occasion for

South Roundabout, model

looking at the situation of public art generally, which is in similar disarray. An airport was a perfect late-twentieth-century case study—teeming with transience and cross-purposes and disarray. In fact the whole challenge was so vast it was almost forbidding.

"For a good while, though, I'd been longing for something exactly like this. I mean, I'd been stumbling along, doing relatively small projects here and there, picking up all these little insights along the way. And Miami was now affording me an opportunity to take stock. It was a little like making the transition from doing little paintings to doing big paintings. It can be a very scary prospect. But one day you just have to take a big canvas, tack it to the wall, and take a whack at it. And that's what Miami became for me."

Fuller had by now moved on to other venues, but Irwin convinced her successor Cesar Trasobares and the airport's director Dick Judy to allow him to invite two of his long-time friends and collaborators, Coy Howard and Ed Wortz, in for a visit. The three of them holed up in the airport hotel for a week roaming the facility, exploring the city, analyzing the situation and dissecting its possibilities.

Part of the challenge was that of airport architecture itself. "Have you ever noticed how there've been hardly any successful airport structures over the past several decades," Irwin asked me, "especially when you compare what's been built with the achievement of railroad architecture toward the end of the last century? Several of those urban train stations, with their wonderful vaulted interiors, were incredible buildings—the girding, the light, the sense of space, *the sense of occasion*. Trains were wonderfully powerful metaphors—the sense of time and distance and journey, of setting out and return, of anticipation and adventure—and the architecture gloried in all that. Maybe when air travel first began it had some of that same sense of adventure to it, but as it developed and became more of a mass-enterprise, most people actually were afraid of flying, and it's as if the architecture became keyed to downplaying and disguising and even masking the essential nature of the experience. The buildings became nondescript, their interiors like shopping malls, or like *living rooms*, for God's sake. It was as if the designers were doing everything possible to keep you from seeing the airplanes as they arrived and departed—you almost had to make a special effort. The entries into the planes themselves were completely swathed in those windowless sheaths—you were in effect invited to move from one living room into another. God forbid you should notice you'd entered a plane. I mean, think about it. Name a single distinguished airport building of the last twenty years. The United Terminal in Chicago, maybe. And what's that? *It's a railway station!*"

Beyond that, Miami had problems of its own. Largely built during the fifties, it was plagued by low ceilings and cramped corridors that tended to defy renovation. It was tremendously crowded, one of the busiest terminals in the country. "Actually,"

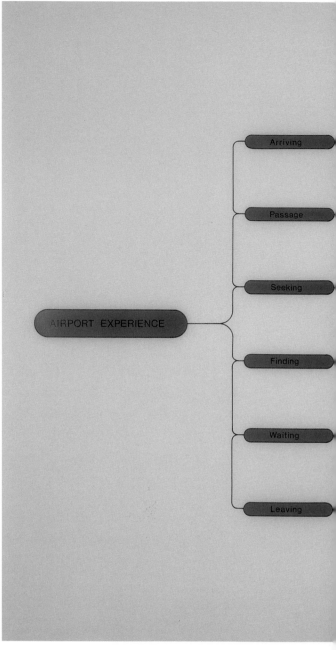

Arts Enrichment Master Plan, proposed 1986 (unrealized) Miami International Airport, Miami, Florida Flow chart developing the interrelated roles of designers, architects, and artists

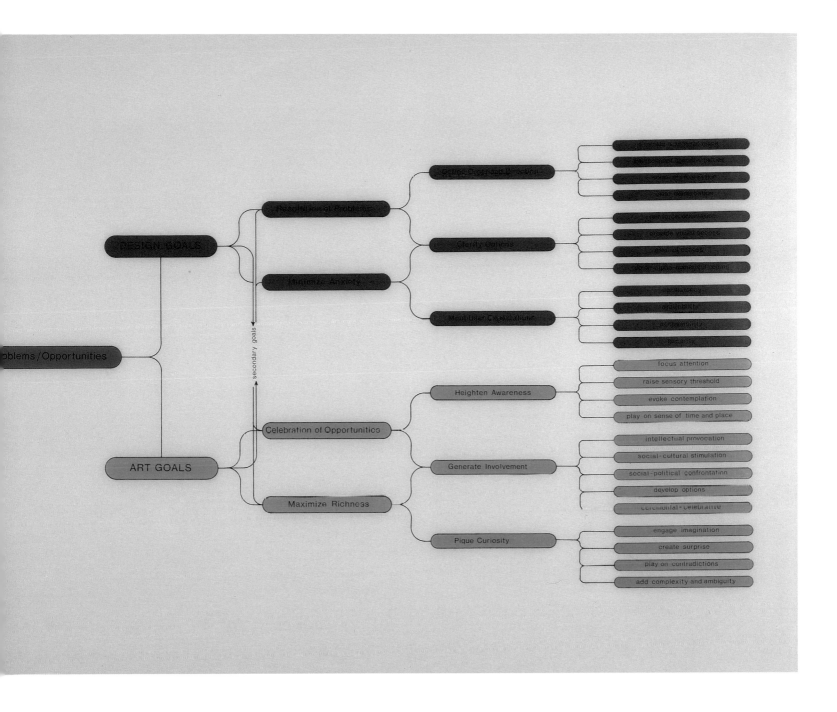

Irwin continued, "it's a terrific people place. You've got the New York-Florida vacation axis. All the people heading out to the Caribbean, or radiating out throughout the Southeast. It's the main air gateway to Latin America, so you've got people going to and from there, making connections to all over the country and on to Europe. For some reason, because of the Latin American connection timetables, there can be unusually long layovers between flights. So you've got all these people just milling around, waiting. A great place for people-watching. Only it's completely disorganized, and it doesn't really lend itself to that sort of activity at all."

Beyond that, like most airports, Miami's is completely without a sense of place. "It could just as well have been in Cleveland," Irwin commented, "for all the local

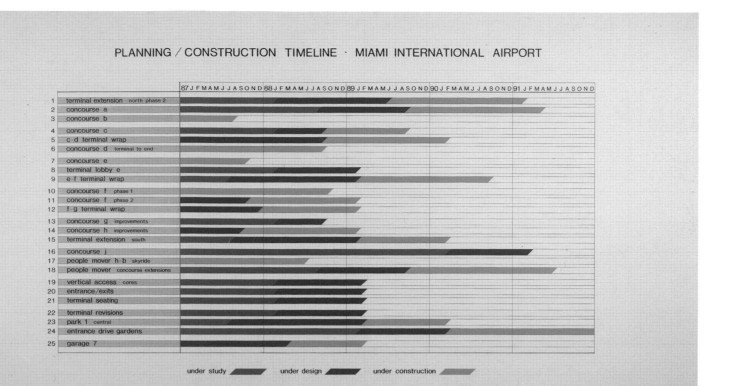

cues it was giving off. I mean, South Florida is one of the richest areas of the country in terms of history and geography and flora and fauna and the quality of the light and general civic liveliness and public myths. Tremendously suggestive. It's just that none of it seems to have suggested anything to the airport's planners."

Irwin and his friends delved deep into the character of the place and spent long hours exploring the character of its opportunities. They broke the airport experience down into six phases—arriving, passage, seeking, finding, waiting, leaving—which tended to repeat themselves again and again in the same sequence, from one zone to the next, across any given transit through the airport (thus, you arrived by car and went through all six phases finding your way into and out of the parking lot; you entered the terminal and repeated the six phases on your way toward the check-in counter, and so forth, to the gate, and then into your plane). Each phase, they came to feel, had a different texture and suggested a different sort of optimal surround (open, for example, versus closed, etc.). Each situation presented both problems and opportunities, and in fact, they noticed, designers and artists seemed to be working at cross-purposes in many of these situations. The architect/designer's main goals were to resolve problems and minimize anxiety, whereas the artist wanted to celebrate opportunities and maximize richness. In actuality, however, each practitioner subsumed the other's goals as his own secondary motives, and the two could complement each other, especially if they were allowed to collaborate from early on. (Irwin went on to elaborate this taxonomy of opportunities in an extraordinarily detailed

Arts Enrichment Master Plan
Construction timeline

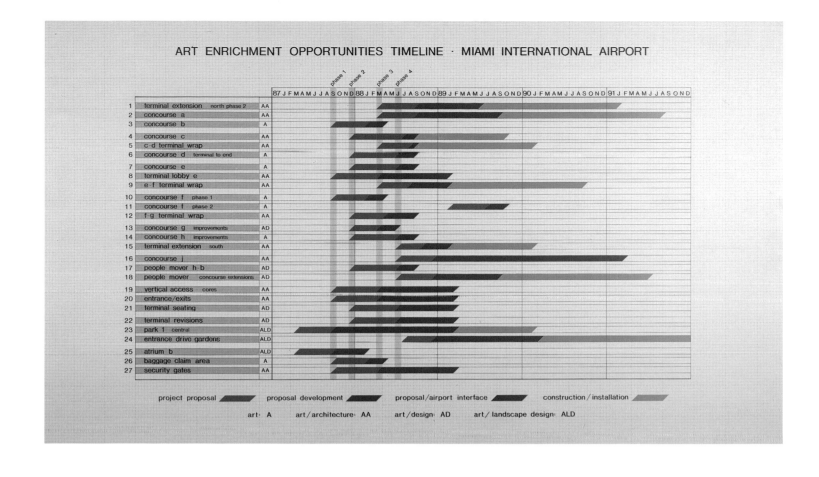

ART ENRICHMENT OPPORTUNITIES TIMELINE · MIAMI INTERNATIONAL AIRPORT

Arts Enrichment Master Plan
"Art Enrichment Opportunities" timeline

chart which he used as the introduction to his eventual presentation to the airport's directors and which he now unscrolled for me.)

"That's the key," Irwin now insisted, jabbing his finger at the chart. "Artists need to be in there from the start, making the argument for quality. The key to this thing, for example, is if you give an engineer a set of criteria which does not include a quality quotient, as it were—that is, if this sense of the quality, the character of the place is not a part of his original motivation—he will then basically put the road straight down the middle. He has no reason whatsoever to curve it. But if I can convince him that quality is absolutely a worthwhile thing and we can then work out a way in which the road can be efficient and also wander down by the river, then we have essentially both—he provides quality in the sense that the road works, I provide quality in that it passes by the river. Now in that way it essentially gets built into the criteria from the start rather than being added on afterwards. In many cases it may not cost any more, or just a bit more, for the road to wander by the river. As opposed to, say, giving the artist one percent afterwards which is, hell, just tokenism to the nth degree. One percent and you're going to change the quality of this experience? Man, that's a pipedream—not possible. The art people are just kidding themselves: the best they're going to be able to do is put in a few doodads. But if you affect this whole process from the beginning by putting in place some quality criteria—when somebody plans something, they establish the criteria, and if quality is not one of the built-in requirements, it's never going to be an effective part of this.

A Visit with Robert Irwin

163

Now, if you look around and ask yourself who in this society is trained to make this argument for quality, the only ones that I can think of are artists. We're the only ones with no other real rationale for being except developing aesthetics or quality—we have no other function. So our key role in our society right now—what we're really talking here is translating values into dollars—is for artists to make winning arguments for why considerations of quality are absolutely necessary."

Returning to his chart, Irwin suggested that any given location in the airport—baggage claim, the security checks, the corridors, the parking lot kiosks, the check-in counters—partook of different combinations of requirements, and the contributions of designers and artists needed to be blended accordingly. But the opportunities for artistic contribution were enormous, even after the fact.

Irwin worked on his Miami scheme for months and in fact for years—developing arguments, developing specific proposals, and perhaps most crucially, developing the trust of airport officials, and particularly that of the airport director, Dick Judy. "When I first arrived," Irwin said, "I'm sure he wondered, 'who is this guy, this artist, being foisted on me by those crazy art bureaucrats downtown?' What standing could I claim in his eyes? What authority could I command? Nothing. I was nobody. I was worse than nobody: I was an irritant." But over time Irwin did seem to develop Mr. Judy's regard. Judy came to welcome his visits and listen to his arguments ever more intently.

Eventually Irwin presented the arts commission and the airport's board with a detailed three-part proposal. To begin with, he offered an elaborate new master plan, entirely reconceiving and revamping the flow of human traffic through the airport from automotive approach through aerial dispatch and back. He then highlighted dozens of locations throughout this newly conceived facility where individual artists could be invited in to work with designers on ways of enriching the specific qualitative features of each particular site; he outlined a procedure for identifying appropriate artists and matching artists to sites; and he prepared a sheaf of impressionistic memos to be sent to each of the participating artists, offering detailed information (and inspiration) on everything from South Florida history to climate conditions, quality of light, diversity of native flora, and so forth. Finally, he selected a single site for himself, in many ways the linchpin of the entire conception: He was proposing to tear out the fairly dilapidated two-story parking garage at the center of the entire facility, surrounded by the entries to all the various terminals, and to replace it with a lush cypress grove. The grove would be layered, with fabulously varied native ferns and birds rising from the marshy lake below—meanwhile, arcing through the

Arts Enrichment Master Plan
Site condition

canopy, pedestrian skyways would link the terminals to each other and to the relocated parking structure beyond. There would be benches and cafes, zones for quiet contemplation during those long layovers.

His audience looked, on that day, slightly aghast at the sheer scale of their assigned artist's vision. "I told them," he told me, as he unfurled several detailed drawings of his proposed grove, "I said, this garden, for example, seems like a major commitment. In all sorts of ways it seems like an extravagance. But if, back in the planning stages, I'd proposed that you take Manhattan and block off the area between 59th and 110th Streets, between Fifth and Eighth Avenues, and put a *park* there, you'd be similarly appalled. You'd tell me: impossible, too costly, utterly impractical, out of the question. But, if I'd then said, 'You have to do it. That park will be the heart, the very lungs of the entire city; it will be the quality, the character of the whole place. You don't have a choice'—eventually you might just have come around."

In his master plan, details of which Irwin continued unscrolling for me, he'd salted all sorts of mini-parks all around the airport—one in the midst of each outward-jutting concourse, for instance—and he proposed matching artists with downtown tourist amenities—aquaria, zoos, parks, etc.—that might value an outpost at the airport. Of course there wasn't any question of trying to realize the entire conception all at once. Certain opportunities could doubtless present themselves almost immediately, and for hardly any money. "The airport has hundreds of windows already, right now," Irwin pointed out, "hardly any of them in any way planned or tended to. What would it be like if we were to invite in some artists to treat the whole lot of them as an array of pictorial opportunities?" (It would, it occurred to me, be like the opposite of the Renaissance.) "Bigger projects could wait. The thing about an airport is that it's in a continuous state of expansion and renovation. The point would be, from here on out, always to include artists from the earliest stages of the planning of each new addition or revision."

Throughout Irwin's time at Miami, he was continuously having to buck bureaucrats with entirely different agendas. "They had one guy there," Irwin recalled, "a city person whose job was 'liability management'—in other words, insurance. Everything had to go across his desk—sewage, road construction, lighting, baggage retrieval—and his job was to make sure the city was never liable. And now here I was, coming along with this—what?—with *art*, for heaven's sake. Let me tell you: we shared no interests whatsoever. His principal interest was in seeing that nothing got done." But Dick Judy, for his part, was becoming increasingly intrigued.

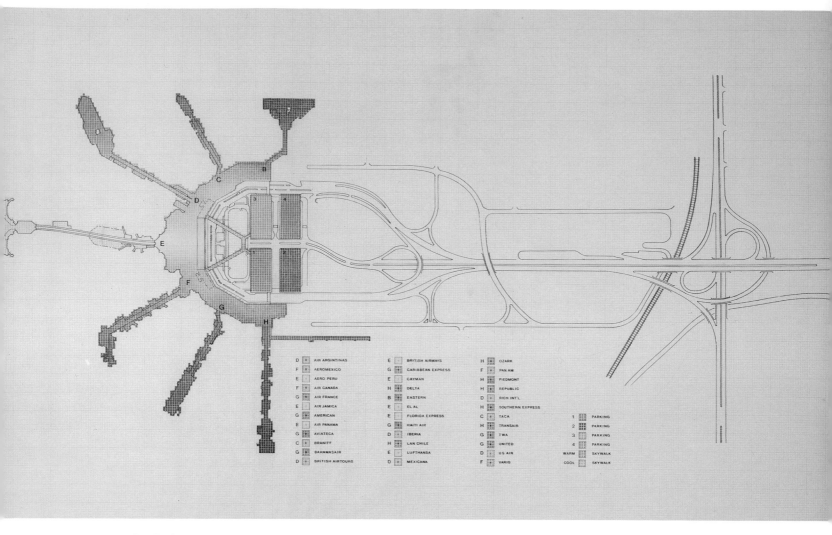

D	AIR ARGINTINAS	E	BRITISH AIRWAYS	H	OZARK		
F	AEROMEXICO	G	CARIBBEAN EXPRESS	F	PAN AM		
E	AERO PERU	E	CAYMAN	H	PIEDMONT		
F	AIR CANADA	H	DELTA	H	REPUBLIC		
G	AIR FRANCE	B	EASTERN	D	RICH INT'L		
E	AIR JAMICA	E	EL AL	H	SOUTHERN EXPRESS		
G	AMERICAN	E	FLORIDA EXPRESS	C	TACA	1	PARKING
E	AIR PANAMA	G	HAITI AIR	H	TRANSAIR	2	PARKING
G	AVIATECA	D	IBERIA	G	TWA	3	PARKING
C	BRANIFF	H	LAN CHILE	G	UNITED	4	PARKING
G	BAHAMASAIR	E	LUFTHANSA	D	US AIR	WARM	SKYWALK
D	BRITISH AIRTOURS	D	MEXICANA	F	VARIG	COOL	SKYWALK

Arts Enrichment Master Plan
Terminal Color Coding Master Plan

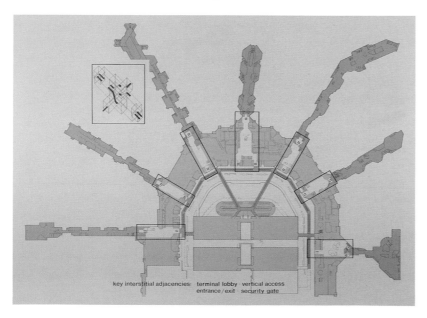

Diagram indicating interstitial adjacencies
Concourse/terminals

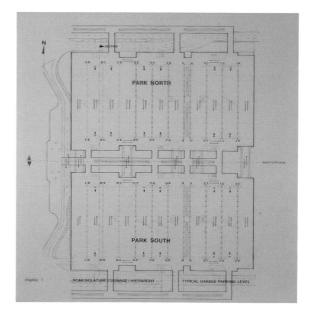

Garage Coding and Nomenclature Plan

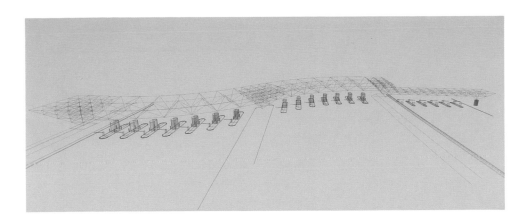

Toll Plaza/Space Frame

"Toll Plaza Garden" Master Plan

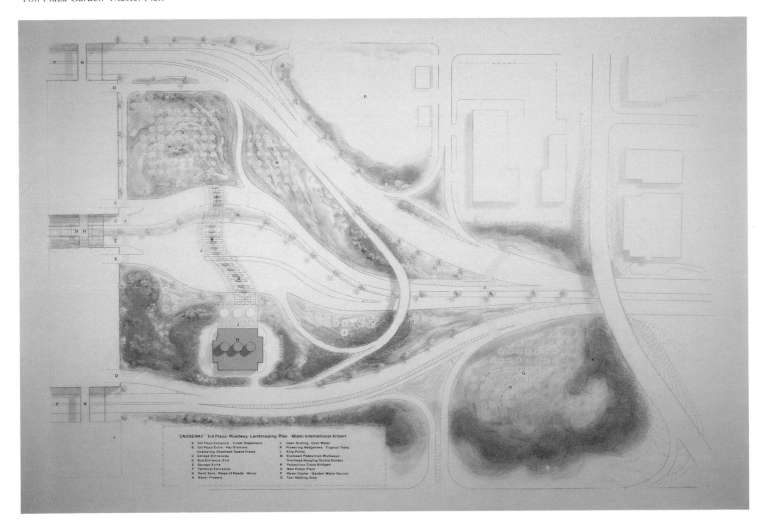

"CAUSEWAY" Toll Plaza · Roadway · Landscaping Plan · Miami International Airport

A   Toll Plaza Entrance · Ticket Dispensers
B   Toll Plaza Exits · Pay Stations
     Undulating Overhead Space Frame
C   Garage Entrances
D   Bus Entrance · Exit
E   Garage Exits
F   Terminal Entrance
G   Sand Bars · Rows of Reeds · Water
H   Water Flowers

J   Open Grating · Over Water
K   Flowering Hedgerows · Tropical Trees
L   King Palms
M   Enclosed Pedestrian Walkways
N   Overhead Hanging Orchid Garden
O   Pedestrian Cross Bridges
P   Water Cooler · Garden Water Source
Q   Taxi Holding Area

He gave Irwin the go-ahead for a first group of artists, including Alexis Smith, Richard Fleischner, Joseph Kosuth, and Coy Howard, to visit the airport and to develop proposals. By 1990, he even seemed on the verge of giving a go-ahead for the entire scheme.

And then, naturally, this veteran of over twenty years running the airport—one of the top people in the international airport managers association—got fired. Or rather, he "resigned" on principle and under pressure, over an entirely different set of issues (a general showdown between the airport and city politicians over control of the airport's finances and revenues). Three years of Irwin's painstaking cultivation of respect and regard were suddenly rendered irrelevant, and the project quickly came unravelled.

"So that was that," Irwin commented, with a sigh, as he began rolling the various diagrams and drawings and sliding them back into their canisters. "But it was a useful exercise, and one which really helped me to crystallize my ideas on the future destiny of art in public places and in fact the whole concept of planning. I always make that distinction between public art and art in public places—it's a question of where you put the emphasis, where you locate the source. The question is how you can take art out into the world."

Miami was a staggeringly ambitious proposal, but one of the most astonishing things about it was its distance from the sorts of things Irwin had been doing ten, fifteen, twenty years earlier. Back then he'd dismantled the art act just about down to Point Zero—he'd gone around saying that the way a tree's shadow fell across a swath of lawn was now art enough for him. He might frame that dapple with a piece of string, but really the piece of string was superfluous. And now here he was—redesigning entire airports.

Could he have stopped, I asked him, back there at Point Zero? Would that ever really have been enough?

Arts Enrichment Master Plan
Elevation drawing,
"Cypress Garden/Central Park"

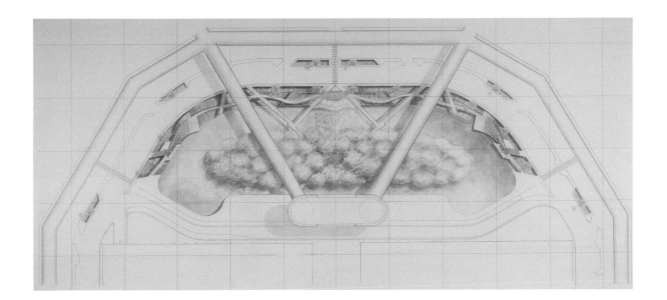

"Oh, absolutely," he replied, without a moment's hesitation.

Why hadn't he?

"Everybody responds to their own stimuli. What happened to me, which is why I have all these paradoxes today, is that I responded to the questions. There does come a point where you can simply withdraw from the world. My argument with my friend Ed Wortz at the time—we'd sort of reversed roles: he'd been a NASA scientist when we first met and within a few years he'd dropped out and was running a Zen center—bottom line, our argument, he would say just that: why don't you? And I would say, 'Ed, why do Zen monks teach?' Why do they? If they're in nirvana, what is that need or desire? Well, there's a stimulus there. Simply as human beings in a human context. Let's say I find total nirvana, okay? I'm at Point Zero in a perfect state of mind, with no need to do anything, okay? But I don't live in an enlightened world. So then come the questions which inundate you right away—there are a number of stimuli, a number of possible responses. I could have become a teacher of Zen, of zeroness—which in fact I could have even done with my paintings. I could still be painting those paintings, which is something like what, say, Robert Ryman has done.

"But I was never really interested in zeroness for its own sake. None of it was ever being done as a negation or a denial of the world. Those butterflies"—he pointed to the vitrines mounted on the wall—"it was during that very period that I was collecting them, corresponding with hobbyists all over the world, trading specimens. Amazing subculture. Sixteen hours a day I'd be painting a cadmium yellow line over a cadmium yellow surface. Two lines per surface, seven days a week. At the end of two years, I emerged with ten canvases. And then the dots, even more minimal—no lines whatsoever!— even more backbreaking: physically excruciating work. Nothing but dots. And the entire time I was collecting these butterflies. I always wanted all that richness, I just didn't know yet how to include it. It was never that I was denying it. I was merely holding it in abeyance.

"I ventured into zeroland because I simply responded to the potential latent in a set of questions—the questions of modernism. I'm really interested in them. Without getting into a religious sort of zeal or anything—I really think . . . I don't

Source material for
Arts Enrichment Master Plan
"Cypress Garden/Central Park"

think modernism was an accident. I think it was an absolutely necessary development of civilization. I think that ultimately it constitutes the next level—not the final one—but we're moving toward another level of sophistication in which we still employ all the previous sophistications . . . because that's the critical thing about modernism: it's not a rejection of other ideas, it's simply an extension, an expansion, a compounding toward a greater complexity."

Listening to Bob's answer, I began realizing something about his work's trajectory. The key movement in the history of the past several hundred years of art, as far as he's concerned, the essence of this thing he describes as the upsurge, the *necessary* upsurge of modernism, has been the collapse of figure and ground. Irwin often talks about the historical sequence that led toward that progression in terms of the compression of what was considered the appropriate subject matter for a work of high art—initially God alone, then Christ the man-God, then Christ the King, then this particular king, then this rich burgher, then the burgher's maidservant in her red shawl, then the red shawl by itself, and eventually just the color red.[1] Toward the end of this five-hundred-year compression, he argues, the subject and its surround, the figure and ground, themselves began collapsing into one another, a process which culminated in, and was the very essence of, the triumph of Cubism. But this wasn't accomplished through a bleaching-out of the figure in which that figure became as undifferentiated as the ground around it. Rather, the ground was being heightened, was suddenly being attended to with all the focus previously reserved for the figure alone. The zone of focus—the allowance for complexity—was being widened.

At a key moment in his own career (somewhere between the dots and the discs), Irwin began to feel that such an ambition, such a dazzling achievement,[2] could no longer be confined to or contained within the world inside the painting alone: doing so was merely rendering the painting figure to the wall's ground, whereas the whole point was to expand the viewer's capacity for complexity still further. In this sense, Irwin reasoned, the shadow the painting was casting had to be every bit as interesting, as loaded, phenomenally speaking, as anything going on inside the painting. Hence his own move out of the frame, onto seemingly blank walls and presently into near-empty rooms, construed as spheres for sublime aesthetic contemplation (or, rather, prior-to-contemplation: sublime attention, presence). The rooms weren't in fact empty, or at any rate, innocent of significant intrusion—their dimensions and lighting and textures had all been modulated in subtle ways which, ideally, heightened the observer's own sense of awareness, without necessarily calling attention to themselves in any way. But the problem remained: the entire room still read as a heightened figure amidst the rest of the world's ground.

It was by way of this progression that Irwin himself approached Point Zero, that moment of virtual self-effacement in terms of his conception of himself-as-an-artist, as a maker of objects, or even as a meddler in rooms. By now he was simply able to go out into the desert and experience a vista, without lifting a finger, without budging a pebble—and that experience, as far as he was concerned, enjoyed in all its richness and for all its complexity, contained every single requisite element of the art act. He could come back into the city and delight himself in the way a random shadow fell across a swath of lawn, savoring it to the point of total immersion. That was enough: that was more than more than enough.

Ten years later, though, and here Irwin was, lifting mountains, revamping entire airports, talking about recasting entire cities. How to account for the change, this seemingly flagrant contradiction? In a certain sense, hourglasslike, he'd simply come out the other side, and his ambitions had become as megalomaniacal as they'd previously been spare. But in another sense—and this is what I now realized—the pro-

gression had been seamless, continuous, and it all had to do with this business of figure and ground. Because coming out the other side didn't so much mean renouncing focus on the discrete art object (the figure—even the entire room as figure) as it meant pumping up awareness of that object's surround, which is to say, *engaging* the whole world, tending to *it* with all the intensity normally reserved for art objects. This is how self-effacement becomes almost messianic in its ambitions. It's not just, with Blake, that if we could only cleanse the doors of perception, we would see the world as it is—infinite. Rather, we would start *making* it infinite. We wouldn't be able to help ourselves: we would become artists of the whole ground—the world entire.

But softly—at least in Irwin's case—softly. "If you asked me the sum total—what is your ambition?" he was continuing. "Basically it's just to make you a little more aware than you were the day before of how beautiful the world is. It's not saying that I know what the world should look like. It's not that I'm rebuilding the world. Basically what artists do is to teach you how to exercise your own potential—they always have, that's the one thread that goes all the way through. I mean, within that there are other strains—the Christian, say, or the Communist—where they claim to know somehow (and this is not even bad, on the best level, it's well-meant), to somehow know how the world should be, and then they try to build it based on some theory, which to me is a peculiar idea, like building your past into your future. What I'm saying is, God, it's all already out there. The whole game is about attending and reasoning. In other words, you have to PLAY IT AS IT LAYS and KEEP IT IN PLAY. Playing it as it lays and keeping it in play means you try to turn people onto themselves, at every moment making it as good as you can make it, but then *they're* responsible. You try to make the best of whatever the moment is, *but this is not an enlightened world*.

"With any new situation, all you're trying to do is to tease out something of significance. You're not trying to form it from the outside, you're just trying to tease it out. If you can get it happening, people will respond, but they'll each respond differently. The point is, you're not trying to control that response. I have no interest in how people respond to the work. It's none of my business. They will respond in an incredible number of ways, and I have no interest in controlling it. I'm not trying to create a feedback loop. I'm just trying to make it as intriguing as I can, and I just assume people will participate. All I'm trying to do is to turn them on to themselves. When the work works at its best, that's what it does: turns people on to themselves."

Turns people on to the world ("just to make you a little more aware than you were the day before of how beautiful the world is")—but particularly on to the most beautiful thing in the world: the human capacity for perception itself.

The ambition is at once phenomenally spare and incredibly vast. As is Irwin's own ego within that ambition: he himself merely wants to do the tiniest thing, which in turn just happens to be the only thing that matters. And it's not even that he himself wants to do it. In his conversation, "I" and "you" regularly blur ("you're not trying to form it from the outside")—and this is no mere rhetorical evasion. The dialogue of immanence, as he calls it, (the sense that "certain questions become demanding and potentially answerable at a certain point in time, and that everyone involved on a particular level of asking questions, whether he's a physicist or a philosopher or an artist, is essentially involved in asking the same questions");[3] the project of inquiry, as he also calls it, this sense that people at the peripheries of their respective disciplines are all engaged in pursuing the same subject (and that every single person, at any moment, has the capacity to transport him or herself to that periphery)—these categories of activity, of intention, are for Irwin, profoundly egoless. "You," "I," "he," "she" are all one. No signatures necessary—and, in fact, every signature, superfluous.

This egolessness of Irwin's, however, can at times seem positively egomaniacal. For instance, a few minutes later we were talking about this whole business of having a retrospective at all. I reminded him of something he'd said to me over ten years ago. At the time we'd been talking about the destruction of two of his dot paintings at the 1965 São Paulo Bienal (their tart self-abnegation had evidently really pissed some viewers off), and he'd commented:

"I suppose if I'd been in São Paulo while they were attacking the things, if I'd been right there, chances are I might have reacted strongly. But it had no reality for me. I mean, I'm told that some work I did a few years back is destroyed. Okay, conceptually I can say, 'Oh God, there goes so many months' work, and there's my economics for the next year, and there goes my place in the world historically.' You can run those through your head and respond to them if you want. But they have no actuality, or didn't for me. I suppose I'm a terrible stepfather to the things I've done, but as far as I'm concerned, I have no children in the world. I can intellectualize that maybe they should be preserved. But I have a hard time assuming the importance of the thing. That's a big difference between a West Coast artist and a European. A European artist really believes in himself as part of that historical tradition, that archive. They see themselves as part of the stream of history, and they conduct themselves in that way, with a certain amount of importance and self-esteem and so forth. I guess people out here have gained that more now, but when I was growing up as an artist there simply wasn't any stream for you to orient yourself toward. Obviously you think what you do is important, or you wouldn't be pursuing it with

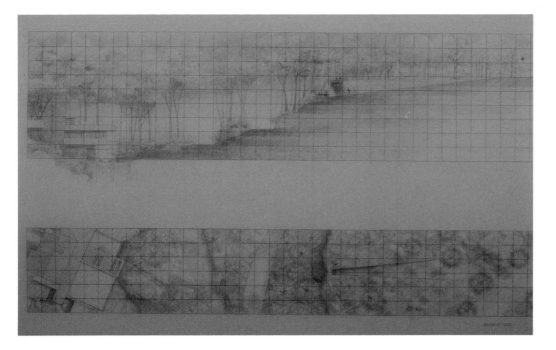

Three Project Sight Lines,
proposed 1988 (unrealized)
Frank Lloyd Wright's "Fallingwater,"
Millrun, Pennsylvania

The invitation to consider a project for
"Fallingwater" was extended by the owner,
Walter Kauffman. After reviewing Wright's
original drawings and spending extensive time
at the site, three important considerations
emerged: 1. The principal elevation of the
house was not really accessible; 2. The most
photographed view of the house, seen from
below the falls, was dangerous to access; 3.
The important view of the house as it steps up
the hill has never really been seen by visitors.

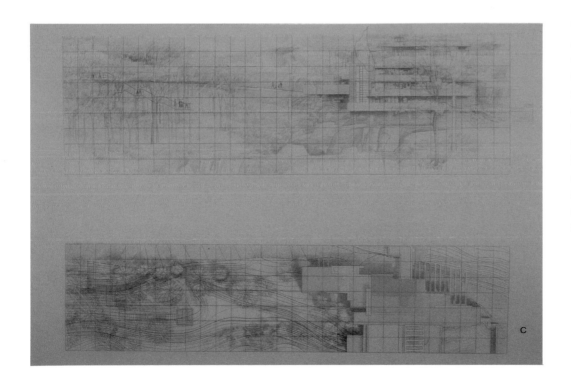

Three Project Sight Lines proposed a series of
unique interactions with the site. **Rock Ledge**
was to be accessed through cuts down and
through the rock face opposite the facing elevation of the house; **Water Walk** was to create
access down the slippery rock face by the
waterfall and a "walk on water" to the ideal spot
for viewing the house over the falls; and **Tree
Walk** accessed the stepped view of the house by
a "catwalk" through the tops of the trees. All
three structures were to be of stainless steel with
open grid surfaces, which would visibly break
up in the pattern of leaves and light.

the kind of intensity you do. But the minute I start thinking about making gestures about my historic role, I mean, I can't do it, I have to start laughing, because there's a certain humor in that."[4]

Given all that, I asked, why bother with a retrospective at all? He was silent for a moment, and then responded: "One thing about the retrospective—maybe this is an illusion of my own making—but I saw an exhibition one time in New York of Mondrian's entire career, and the thing that was amazing to me was that there was the full span of his career, from the flowers on out to the most incredible abstractions, and Mondrian was one of those few rare artists in which, a) there was this tremendous growth and change, and b) at the same time, every step of it was there. I mean, pfew!—you could just see it, you could see how each step evolved from the one before, how there wasn't any revolution, it was all a process of continually considered evolution, one that took him, step by step, all the way out.

"And I just have a feeling that my work has some of the same character: I've gone a fairly long distance and done it step by step, every step is there, exhibited. Maybe it's a bit more difficult to see, since it's not all in one medium, but it's all there."

He paused, gazing out at the bay. A destroyer was cruising in silently, spinnakers frolicking soundlessly about it. "And then there's this business of leaving a decent record. I mean, I'm in a pretty hilarious position in that most of my work of the past twenty years doesn't exist—most of it was never even built, and for the craziest variety of reasons. My proposal for Frank Lloyd Wright's Fallingwater: the guy dies. My towers for Chicago: the company goes broke—a major fucking insurance company, we're all ready to go, I've even managed to bring the thing in under budget, and suddenly, wham!—the company's in Chapter Eleven. My proposal for the French Olympics: complete failure of communication—I'm offering them this delicate wispy gesture and their people start engineering the thing to death, I'm offering them a butterfly and they're engineering me an elephant; no wonder it falls through. Miami: the guy gets fired. I mean, it can get pretty comical. Here I am with this aesthetic utterly rooted in experience and the pieces don't even exist.

"Up till now I haven't cared all that much. I mean, as you documented with that quote, I didn't use to give history, or anyway my own place in history, all that much thought. But I'm increasingly coming to realize that the kind of thing I'm really interested in, I'm never going to see in my lifetime. Even if I still have another twenty good years ahead of me, I can see that the kind of vision and practice I'm working toward is generations off. Now, the previous generation left me a great record to work from—Mondrian, de Kooning. . . . I didn't have to spend a lifetime coming to know them—the record was there, waiting for me when I was ready to assimilate it. Whereas my stuff, my offering, for the most part simply isn't going to be there to pass on because, without meaning to sound grandiose about it, almost all my more recent steps have essentially been erased.

"And I guess I just feel that one has a responsibility as a human being to leave a good record. If I'd never seen a de Kooning except in a magazine, I'd have been

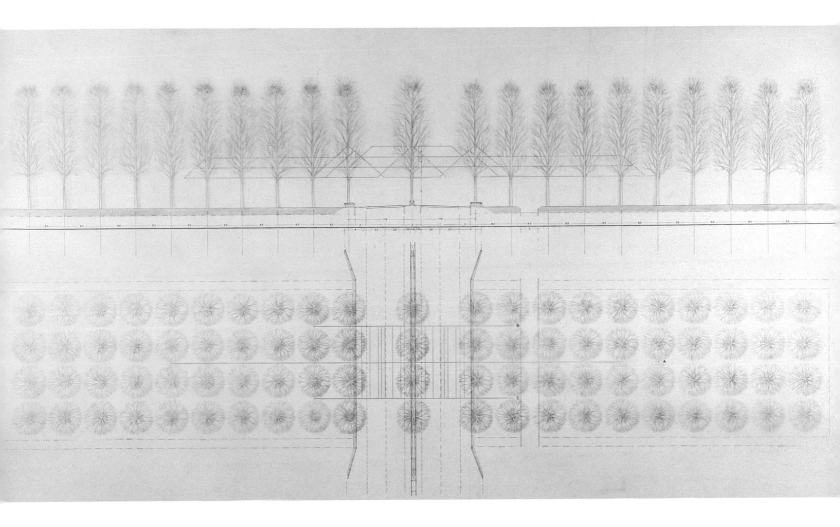

Allée, proposed 1990
(unrealized)
Rhône-Alps, France
Sponsored by the French
Ministry of Culture

Quaking aspen trees, Kolorgaard
plastic-coated yellow and orange
mesh fencing

Allée frames the entrance to the
Rhône Valley and Albertville,
France, site of the 1992 Winter
Olympics. Quaking aspen trees
flank the road, and layered orange
and yellow mesh fencing forms a
"covered bridge."

operating from a bad record. Or like in *The Double Helix*—why were Watson and
Crick able to beat Pauling to the discovery of DNA? Because they had the lady's
photographs and he didn't. They were working from better information."

He paused again, puzzling it all through. "Obviously, in a certain sense, doing a
retrospective is a big step backwards for me. I want to be over here—beyond
Miami—and instead I'm back here, back in the very museums and galleries I
foreswore a long time ago. But it's all part of the same crazy contradiction of my
entire enterprise these days. Because not only do the projects I want to do in the
outside world generally fall through for one reason or another, but my ties to my
source, to the art world, are also beginning to fray. I'm doubly estranged: I fall
between: I've become invisible to both worlds. And this retrospective is finally about
the art world. It's about the fact that despite my energy's being focused over here,
still I remain tethered to my source, which is in the art world. And part of the thing
about a tether is that when your tether gets tangled up, you've got real problems, it
starts spinning you in all sorts of bad directions, you'd better tend to it. Furthermore,
you can only go as far as people are willing to entertain you. I can have the most far-
out ideas, but if absolutely no one else takes them seriously, in a sense I'm operating
in a vacuum. One of the reasons I taught all those years"—Irwin was referring to the
period during the seventies when, having abandoned his studio, he was on the road
virtually continuously, making himself "available in response" as he called it at the

time, lecturing and visiting with any art schools that would have him[5]—"is that it's very important that we all participate in the health of our disciplines. Whether or not I can get myself to take history seriously, I do take the health of my discipline very seriously. Disciplines can shrivel up and die if they're not properly tended. So that, yes, with this whole retrospective exercise, I'm no longer pursuing the questions; but this sort of contribution is important as well. It's like the way Einstein sat down at one point and wrote a primer. At that point he was no longer developing his own knowledge, but he was accepting the fact that he was a human being in a human context and had some interest and some responsibility."

I mentioned the way that Valéry's "Seeing is forgetting . . ." aphorism had once served as apt characterization of his entire course up to a certain point. How would he encapsulate the period since? What would be a good title for the retrospective?

"You know," he replied, "oddly something came to mind the other day—maybe not exactly what you have in mind but I think it sums up the trajectory nicely: From Malevich to Tatlin. Those Russian Constructivists—spectacular moment, tremendous burst of creative energy. In a way the work itself was quite crude—it's like I always say: as the questions go up, the performance level goes down (which is natural, people don't yet know how to act on those questions, they're stumbling around in a fog), whereas when performance goes up, the quality of the questions usually tends to go down. So, while the objects these guys came up with may not have been particularly sophisticated as objects—they weren't Stellas or anything—they were absolutely loaded in other ways. Man, we're still feeding off their questions. Those guys were *soaring*.

"Malevich, of course, pared everything down to that empty white square. Everybody saw that and moaned, 'Ooooh nooo, everything we love is gone.' And instead he replied, 'Ah, but we have found a desert of pure feeling!' Incredibly philosophical thing to say. One could easily have equated that empty square with the loss of God, the end of culture, the horror of death—and there's a whole artistic tradition that in effect does that: the existentialist tradition.[6] But I'm convinced Malevich was drawing on the opposite tradition, the phenomenological.[7] Instead of angst, he's telling you Wonder! Wow! A desert of pure feeling! And he's not talking about emotion, or anyway not just about emotion. He's talking about texture, about experience, about quality, about taking the *feel* of things." For a moment I recalled the way Irwin used to talk about placing bets at the horse races (his principal livelihood back in the old days)—how he'd always start out by carefully surveying the quantifiable data, and how he'd then blend in the more subtle, nonquantifiable, more intuitive kinds of information, and how then he'd run his hand over the entire race, trying to get *a feel for the whole,*

Kasimir Malevich
Suprematist Composition:
White on White, 1918
Oil on canvas
31 1/4 x 31 1/4 inches
The Museum of Modern Art,
New York

and how only then would he make his stab and place his wager.[8] (In a way it's the same sort of procedure he still deploys whenever he approaches each new artistic situation.) "See, Malevich was keying on experience. His was a desert in which experience is primary. If God is primary, then how you construct every argument is always referenced back to God, because that's the primary thing. But when he says, 'a desert of pure feeling,' how I interpret that is he's saying, 'I am primary, the human being is primary, and I reference everything back to me.' We're not talking about the thing, but rather the source of the thing—the responsibility of the observer, the perceiver. This was a profoundly philosophical moment and he was acting it all out inside his studio, within the confines of his canvas. And what Tatlin was doing at that exact same moment, he was trying to take that way of being out in the world, trying to fashion a thing-in-the-world based on that same euphoric sense of human potential. Sure, it was purely a gesture, and by the way one of the oldest gestures there is, one of the oldest metaphors: a Tower. Ever since human beings have stood on the earth, they've been building mounds and towers. But it was just like with the square: a pure gesture in the same way the square is a pure gesture. A gesture about soaring possibility. for a brief moment, all the chains were off and the human spirit was soaring.

"Now, of course, in one sense they're the same, the square and the tower, but in another sense it's a big trip, it's a real journey. Because how exactly do you take that white square—that 'desert of pure feeling'—and project its spirit out into the world? In a sense my dot paintings were my Malevich equivalents, and the things I'm trying to do now are my Tatlin equivalents."[9]

Malevich, Tatlin—I found myself thinking—Mondrian, de Kooning, Einstein, Watson, Crick. Fairly pricey neighborhood in which Irwin keeps insisting on pitching his tent. But again, his is a strangely egoless egomania: in claiming these masters as his colleagues, he's not so much keying on his own importance as asserting the importance of the ongoing dialogue. Irwin's is an immensely playful sensibility, but the play is absolutely serious. If he alludes to Einstein and Watson, he's merely insisting that art has both the right and the obligation to stake its claims as high as any science. And if he mentions Mondrian or Malevich, he's merely insisting that artists today—the entire discipline—ought cast their aspirations right up there with the heroes. Play it as it lays, and keep it in play.

"And as I've been showing you," Irwin was continuing, gesturing over to the pile of scrolled diagrams and blueprints, "it's not that easy a trip, it's by no means obvious. I mean, as long as you confined it to the studio, where you had it in a kind of laboratory circumstance, you could limit the paradoxes, make the world appear any way you wanted it to, so long as you didn't expect

Vladimir Tatlin (after)
Model for the Monument to the Third International, 1920
Reconstructed 1983 by Smithsonian Institution Office Exhibits Central and the Hirshhorn Museum and Sculpture Garden

anybody to agree. But the minute you put it under your arm and take it outside, you immediately run aground of all sorts of paradoxes—both the physical limitations and the limitations imposed by everybody else's ambitions and requirements. The invitations I get nowadays are not invitations to do what I want to do. My invitations come from people who have their own reasons and assumptions—not mine. As of course they would—no reason why it should be any different. But from the outset we're in total contradiction. It's a bit like the scientist in his lab developing, say, superconductivity. Under perfect lab conditions he can freeze the fucker way down and, wow!, just look at that thing levitate in midair! But that's a long way from making a train levitate and race along its tracks, and in the meantime there are all sorts of contradictions—it doesn't work, and people don't necessarily want it. Till it's proven, who needs it? In a way, with this retrospective I've momentarily retreated halfway back into the lab."

The trouble, I pointed out, is that the retrospective is itself not without its contradictions—not the least of which being the absurd limitations imposed by the necessary substitution of models and photos and wall renderings in lieu of actual physical experience.

"Of course!" Irwin immediately concurred. "Of course. And on top of that, these are models of pieces in radically different media—light and sound, dirt, steel and glass, scrim, transported boulders, chainlink, cacti and bougainvillea. At each of the retrospective's stops I'll be erecting at least one site-conditioned piece, but they will all be entirely different, each responding to the conditions of its specific site. And what are people going to think? Only two things they can think. The first would be to assume, from any normal art world perspective, that I'd gone totally eclectic, I've completely lost my rudder, I'm simply stealing ideas from everybody in sight. Or else—and maybe a few people will entertain me this far—they might take me seriously and assume that an entirely different aesthetic is operating here, and if so, they might ask themselves, what could it be?[10]

"I mean, in undertaking a retrospective at all I had to accept the idea of a dialogue with the art world in all its peculiarities. And it's a little bit like that book *Flatland*, you know, where the author meticulously sets out this two-dimensional world, and then he introduces a visitor from the third dimension. Thing is, everything the visitor shows them can be explained away two-dimensionally. There's no way you can introduce the third dimension to the second that can't be rationalized away. Same thing applies to us here: the idea of the fourth dimension. Basically when you look at the art world on the whole, it's a three-dimensional world—all its structures and practices are geared to three dimensions—and I'm basically trying to introduce a fourth dimension. I mean, I—we—there's a group of us exploring the

Robert Irwin during installation of **1 2 3 4°** at The Pace Gallery, New York, November 1992

1 2 3 4°, 1992
The Pace Gallery, New York

same terrain. And when we do it, there is no fourth-dimension forum, no fourth-dimension language that is commonly spoken. I may not even speak the language that well myself at this stage—okay?—but I'm doing projects that have dimensions on them, ways of going, that when I put them inside a building, I'm trying to cram them back into a three-dimensional world, and they almost disappear. At best, if somebody's paying attention, he or she might just get a brief intimation, a momentary trace, like a streak in a cloud chamber. But that's it."

When Einstein or Heisenberg talk about the fourth dimension, I pointed out, they're talking about time.

"That's what I'm talking about, too," Irwin insisted. "Exactly that. Time: *experience*. Einstein gives you all that stuff about time and trains coming toward you and going away, but it's always in relationship to you as the perceiver, the observer. Time is experience. Time is a nonthing, it has no physical properties—or infinite physical properties. I can point to its effects—the flower opens, the flower closes, the flower dies; or the way a clock metes out time; or the cadences, the rhythms of a voice—but I'm not pointing at time. Time is only understood in here" (he thumped his chest) "or there" (he pointed at mine)" —it's totally experiential. And in the same way, quality—qualities—only reveal themselves to observers, across time."

Paradoxically, it occurred to me, presence itself—Irwin's holy grail—only reveals itself across time, across the fourth dimension. You have to stop, shut up, and listen, if—one, two, three, four, five—you're ever going to hear.

Outside the sun was setting, and evening was coming on.

If you spend any time with Irwin, you're likely to notice that he has two quintessential gestures. He'll be rolling along, expounding at length, and then at a certain moment he'll bring his hand up, thumb and fingers bunched together, like a tulip, which he then proceeds to open out, a blossoming— his whole face opening, his eyebrows riding up his broad forehead, a bemused grin spreading across his face: an easy, breezy gesture of openness and release. You've got to keep your sense of humor, he'll say, at a certain point you've just got to let things go. The tulip, opening. I mean, I can just be sitting there, not much happening, but it's plenty and it's all

I need. The tulip, opening. All I'm saying—the tulip, opening—is that the wonder is still there. Sometimes it gets so good—you know how sometimes, once in a long while, you'll take a piss and afterwards your whole body is *tingling*: that's the effect I'm aiming for. The tulip opening wide.

And then other times, his entire being will seem to focus, to concentrate, his face will scrunch up, his eyes narrow, he'll seem to throw all his body weight behind his arm as it screws an imaginary anchor into an invisible massif before him, a gesture all gritty with determination. In fact, sometimes he'll even grunt—mmmff. I mean, either you're going to do it or you're not going to do it, and if you're going to do it, you've got to get in there and—mmfff—do it. You've got to take all that and somehow, man—mmmff—you've got to nail it. You really have to bite the bullet if you're going to do philosophy, halfway doesn't count for anything and there are no excuses; in the world there are all sorts of excuses, and good ones, for not beating the shit out of yourself; but if you're going to pursue certain lines of thought, take on certain tasks, well—mmmff—you've really got to make the commitment.

I talk about Irwin's contradictions, and in a certain sense this is one of the core ones. Because here's an artist who time and again is trying to nail down beatitude. He wants to take all that bliss, all that serenity, all that wonder, and—damn it, he wants to batten it down. He wants to batten it down tight and then—ppfff· the tulip opening—to just let it go.[11]

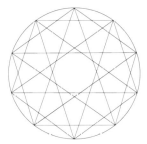 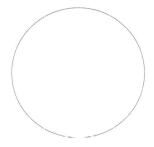

Years ago, when Bob and I were reading philosophy together—as a way of getting to know each other, really—we stumbled upon the formulations of a late medieval neoplatonist theologian and philosopher, a mathematician known as Nicholas of Cusa (1401-1464). Nicholas has this wonderful way of talking about the difference between logic and faith, or alternatively, between knowing and truth. Logic, he suggests, knowing, is like an n-sided polygon inscribed inside a circle. The more sides you add, the more complexities you introduce, the more the polygon approaches the circle which surrounds it. And yet the farther away it gets, as well. For the circle is but a single, seamless line, whereas your polygon seems to be breeding more and more lines, more and more angles, becoming less and less seamless. No matter how many sides you add, no matter how closely the inscribed polygon begins to *approximate* the circle, it never reaches the circle, and at a certain point a leap is required, from the tangent to the arc, from endlessly compounding multiplicity to singleness of being. Another name for that leap, of course, is grace.

Thinking about Irwin's work these days, I often think about Nicholas's formulation. There's all this heavy lifting, this incredible shifting of land and heaving of structure—ever more complex and ambitious—but finally it's all meant to occasion something ineffably simple, and at its best it does: a sense of awareness. A shimmering sense of awareness. The same thing might be said of this entire retrospective exercise. As well, for that matter, as the preposterous exercise of even trying to write about it.

Overleaf: **1 2 3 4°**, 1992, The Pace Gallery, New York

Notes

1. Lawrence Weschler, *Seeing is Forgetting the Name of the Thing One Sees: A Life of Contemporary Artist Robert Irwin* (Berkeley and Los Angeles: University of California Press, 1982), p.109.

2. There are, of course, other readings of the history and significance of the Cubist achievement. Shortly after I completed *Seeing is Forgetting* in 1982, I happened to be invited to write the text for the book of David Hockney's *Cameraworks*. Hockney, too, finds the Cubist moment positively seminal—but his interpretation of its implications is almost the exact opposite of Irwin's. For him, the most profound achievement of Cubism was the way it revitalized the possibilities of figurative depiction.

    "The great misinterpretation of twentieth-century art," he told me, "is the claim advanced by many people, especially critics, that Cubism of necessity led to abstraction, that Cubism's only true heritage was this increasing tendency toward a more and more insular abstraction. But on the contrary, Cubism was about the real world. It was an attempt to reclaim a territory for figuration, for depiction. Faced with the claim that photography had made figurative painting obsolete, the Cubists performed an exquisite critique of photography; they showed that there were certain aspects of looking—basically the *human* reality of perception—that photography couldn't convey, and that you still needed the painter's hand and eye to convey them. I mean, several paths led out from those initial discoveries of Picasso and Braque, and abstraction was no doubt one of them. In that sense, it's a legitimate heir. I've always felt that what was wrong with Tom Wolfe's polemic against the American Abstract Expressionist movement in *The Painted Word* was that he never did understand that those people were sincere. But still you have to ask yourself, why didn't Picasso and Braque, who invented Cubism, ever follow that path? And I suspect that it's because sitting there in Paris back in the early 1910s, playing out the various possibilities in their minds, they could already see

that abstraction led into a *cul-de-sac*, and they didn't need to do it to find out." (Weschler, *David Hockney's Cameraworks*, p.38.) In some ways, I intended that Hockney text (along with a sequel in the catalogue to Hockney's 1988 retrospective) to read as a complete refutation of *Seeing is Forgetting*, which in turn reads as a total refutation of them. Curiously, however, while engaging in entirely different artistic enterprises—undergirded, they would argue, by entirely opposite readings of history—many of Hockney's and Irwin's core concerns are almost identical: the emphasis, for instance, on the *human* quality of looking and experience, the centrality of the observer, the vitality of the periphery, the dialogue of immanence, and even the critique of photography. Hockney once commented to me that he used to find Irwin's onetime prohibition on the photographing of his art works a bit daft and even fetishistic, but that he'd come round to feeling that Irwin had been absolutely right: there was a serious problem with the camera.

3. *Seeing is Forgetting*, p.137.

4. Ibid., pp.95-96.

5. Ibid., pp.163-67.

6. Irwin often talks about the way that his generation of California artists, serenely unbowed by the weight of history, were able to perceive the New York Abstract Expressionist achievement afresh, to strip it, as it were, of its existentialist death-intoxication and to tap into its phenomenological essence, its physicality, its wondrous potential for expressing and occasioning presence.

    Those California artists *were* serenely unbowed by the weight of history, or at any rate Irwin certainly was. I'm reminded of a conversation we had one day years ago as we were driving around his old haunts in the Inglewood section of Los Angeles. He'd been regaling me with tales of the glory days of his youth—the cars, the girls, the dancing, the beach—when at one point we wheeled round by a movie theater. I subsequently included the ensuing conversation in *Seeing is Forgetting* (pp.11-12):

    "Here's the theater I worked at for several years. Next door there was a little restaurant called Tip's, and I'd work there occasionally, too. That parking lot back there, which they shared, is where me and my buddies used to siphon gas out of unsuspecting vehicles. We'd take out the garbage and shift the hoses and cannisters. They were of course rationing in those days."

This was the first time the war had impinged on Bob's recollections. I wondered whether it had had any more significance for him then.

"Oh, no," Bob responded immediately. "We were just oblivious. We conducted ourselves like the war wasn't on in any way. Not having gas and all that was simply a challenge. I didn't have any older brothers, and come to think of it, none of my friends in that group did either. Maybe that was part of it. But basically we didn't pay any attention."

I asked him if the obliviousness of the local youth had bothered the older members of the community, whether he and his friends were criticized as irresponsible.

"I don't know. I mean, if I was oblivious to the war, I was certainly oblivious to any criticism!"

Irwin was thirteen at the time of the Japanese attack on Pearl Harbor, just graduating high school as the war ended. I asked him where he had been December 7, 1941.

"I don't know," he replied.

I asked him about the day the war ended.

"Haven't the slightest idea."

Hiroshima?

"Nope. *Hiroshima Mon Amour* was the story of a fairy tale."

I wondered if part of the reason he and his friends were having such a fiercely good time was because they all realized they were presently going to be shuttled off to the war.

"Oh, no," Bob dismissed the notion with a sweep of his hand. "Look. Look at it here. Look at how it is: calm, sunny, the palm trees. What is there to get all fucking upset about?" He laughed. "This is reality. In other words, the war was not reality. The war wasn't here. The war was someplace else. So any ideas you had about the war were all things you manufactured in your head from newspapers and that. To me, this was reality; this was my reality right here."

7. This sort of construction—with existentialism and phenomenology cast as polar opposites—is vintage Irwin. Irwin didn't begin actually reading philosophy till quite late in his career, in fact well after he'd finished performing an utterly untutored phenomenological reduction of his own painterly vocation, having bracketed himself right out of his studio and into the desert. It was only then, in the late seventies, that he first had recourse, as I recorded in *Seeing is Forgetting* (p.179), to Husserl, Wittgenstein, Sartre, Schütz. . . . It was not the most elegant dialogue. The style of discourse was utterly foreign to Irwin, and his steps were often clumsy, lurching, leaden. He mistook passages, shaved nuances, mauled subtleties. But progressively he improved—and more fundamentally than that, like a craftsman at his lathe, he honed his own thinking. His grappling with these books was not so much an occasion for the correct elucidation of the course of Western philosophy as an adjunct in the continued refining of his own inquiry. In this context it did not matter that he continually called positivists and behaviorists "structuralists" or Maurice Merleau Ponty, "Ponty." What mattered was how he distilled a particular tenor of thinking into his own.

So that, yes, of course, fine: existentialism in fact grows out of phenomenology. Sartre and Heidegger studied under Husserl. Husserl's phenomenology, particularly in its later emanations, is saturated with forebodings of doom—as well it might have been, having been composed during the thirties in Freiburg. Camus's earliest existentialist writings, for their part (composed only shortly thereafter, in the late thirties and forties, though in Algiers), are utterly saturated with a zest for living, a sense of sheer beatific wonder in face of nature's provenance. It pays to be careful when listening to Irwin on philosophy. And yet, at the same time, he *is* on to something fundamental—and certainly something fundamental about his own work, about which these misconstruals afford, to borrow a phrase, a positive map of misreading.

8. *Seeing is Forgetting*, pp.138-46.

9. Guy Davenport, the masterful essayist and professor of English at the University of Kentucky, included an uncannily similar series of meditations on the relationship between Malevich and Tatlin and on the significance of their respective projects, in the title "story" of his splendid first collec-

tion of fictions, *Tatlin!* (Scribners, 1974, and Johns Hopkins University Press, 1982). For example: "Malevich, Tatlin said, prefigures the future. I am the future. Malevich is a kite, I am a glider." (p.37) "We agree that art is a model for living. He [Malevich] is a blueprint, I [Tatlin] am a saw and hammer." (p.39) Elsewhere, Davenport records how "Puni has glued a plate to a tabletop and called it a construct: the cubist guitar. He [Tatlin] can go further. He can identify the full moon in the sky as a cubist guitar." (p.39) Or: "It is, Osip Mandelstam would say in later years, the quality of sunlight on a wall. He was speaking of civilization." (p.9) Or, finally (p.29), Tatlin considering the implications of Picasso: "That's what [his] constructions in paper were: a vocabulary of forms, a model of harmonies and relations. *Art must die and be reborn in everything.*"

10. Compare this formulation, offered by the German-Austrian modernist composer Ernst Toch, during a 1932 Pro Musica Society tour of the United States:

> You must listen without always wanting to compare with the musical basis you already have. You must imagine that you inherited from your ancestors different compartments in the musical part of your brain, just as you inherited any other physical or intellectual qualities. Now when you hear a piece from the pre-classic, classic, or romantic periods, the sounds fall without any trouble and agreeably into the already prepared compartments. But when music for which you have no prepared compartments strikes your ear, what happens? Either the music remains outside you or you force it with all your might into one of those compartments, although it does not fit. The compartment is either too long or too short, either too narrow or too wide, and that hurts you and you blame the music. But in reality you are to blame, because you force it into a compart-

ment into which it does not fit, instead of calmly, passively, quietly, and without opposition, helping the music to build a new compartment for itself.

11. All this reminds me of a conversation I had several years ago with the dealer Irving Blum, who'd co-managed the famed Ferus Gallery in L.A. during those years in the late fifties and early sixties, when Irwin was first showing his Abstract Expressionist and line paintings there. Blum had been describing how extraordinarily driven and competitive Irwin had seemed in those days, and I commented that it was hard to square the "fierce competitiveness" of the Irwin he was describing with the apparent serenity Irwin projects today.

"Well, I don't understand that serenity," Blum confessed. "I don't understand what's beneath it. I just can't believe there isn't still the same kind of endless, agonizing churning that there's always been. I'm suspicious of that serenity, although I've confronted it. It's absolutely different from the way he used to be. I mean, he was a tough competitor—he made no bones about it. And his ambition was, as I say, limitless, which was all very clear upon first meeting him. He believed violently in what he was doing, and it was not that unusual for him to get into physical fights about things he believed in. Now he seems almost tranquil, utterly content . . . and I mistrust that tranquility. I don't know how to deal with it. I just know Irwin as the eye of the hurricane, and I don't understand this new Zen quality."

I pointed out that from his earliest days at Ferus, Irwin had been dealing in Zen themes. "Oh, yes," Blum replied, "always, but he was dealing with Zen in the most aggressive way Zen has ever been dealt with."
Seeing is Forgetting, p.51.

Checklist

Black Raku, 1959
Oil on canvas
71 x 84 inches
Collection of the artist

The Lucky U, 1959 (p. 76)
Oil on canvas
71 x 84 inches
Estate of Helen Jacobs

Form for Tomorrow, ca. 1959-60
Oil on canvas in wood frame
15 1/2 x 15 inches
Collection of Dr. and Mrs. Merle S. Glick,
Los Angeles

Untitled, ca. 1959-60 (p. 80)
Oil on canvas in wood frame
11 1/4 x 11 1/2 inches
Collection of the artist

Untitled, ca. 1959-60 (p. 81)
Oil on canvas in wood frame
11 5/8 x 11 1/2 inches
Collection of the artist

Untitled, ca. 1959-60
Oil on canvas in wood frame
15 1/4 x 15 1/4 inches
Collection of the artist

Untitled, ca. 1959-60
Oil on canvas in wood frame
20 3/4 x 20 3/4 inches
Collection of the artist

Untitled, ca. 1959-60 (p. 54)
Oil on canvas in wood frame
20 3/4 x 21 inches
Collection of the artist

Form for Tomorrow, 1960 (p. 83)
Oil on canvas in wood frame
16 1/8 x 15 1/2 inches
Courtesy of Margo Leavin, Los Angeles

Lucky U, 1960 (p. 82)
Oil on canvas in wood frame
15 1/2 x 15 1/2 inches
Private collection, courtesy of Joni Gordon,
Newspace, Los Angeles, and Adrienne Fish,
871 Fine Art, San Francisco

Ocean Park, ca. 1960-61 (p. 86)
Oil on canvas
65 1/2 x 65 1/8 inches
Collection of the artist

Pier I, 1960
Oil on canvas
65 3/4 x 65 inches
Collection of Richard and Frances Luban,
Los Angeles

Pier I, ca. 1960-61 (p. 87)
Oil on canvas
65 1/2 x 65 1/8 inches
Collection of the artist

Pier II, ca. 1960-61
Oil on canvas
66 x 65 inches
Collection of Mr. and Mrs. Donn Chappellet,
St. Helena, California

Untitled, 1960 (p. 84)
Oil on canvas in wood frame
15 3/16 x 15 3/16 inches
Collection of Roberta Neiman, Los Angeles

The Four Blues, 1961 (p. 55)
Oil on canvas
65 5/8 x 65 1/8 inches
San Francisco Museum of Modern Art
Purchased with the aid of a gift of Rena Bransten
(Los Angeles only)

Band in Boston, 1962
Oil on canvas
66 x 65 inches
Los Angeles County Museum of Art
Los Angeles County Fund

A Bed of Roses, 1962
Oil on canvas
66 x 65 inches
Private collection

Bowl of Cherries, 1962
Oil on canvas
65 5/8 x 65 1/8 inches
Private collection
(Paris and Madrid only)

Crazy Otto, 1962 (p. 100)
Oil on canvas
66 x 65 inches
The Pace Gallery, New York

The Ideal Spot, ca. 1962
Oil on canvas
66 1/8 x 65 1/8 inches
Collection of Mr. and Mrs. Abraham Ratner,
San Diego
(Paris and Madrid only)

Jake Leg, 1962 (p. 98)
Oil on canvas
66 x 65 inches
Collection of Earl Lewis Goldberg,
Brentwood, California

Matinee Idol, 1962 (p. 101)
Oil on canvas
66 1/8 x 65 1/8 inches
The Museum of Contemporary Art, Los Angeles
Given in memory of Gene Burton
by Laura-Lee and Robert Woods

Untitled, 1962
Oil on canvas
82 1/2 x 84 1/2 inches
Museum of Contemporary Art, San Diego
Museum purchase with
funds from the Bobby Short Benefit

Untitled, 1962-63 (p. 102)
Oil on canvas
82 1/2 x 84 1/2 inches
Norton Simon Museum, Pasadena
Gift of the artist, 1969

Untitled, 1962-64
Oil on canvas
82 1/2 x 84 1/2 inches
Collection of Edward and Melinda Wortz,
Pasadena

Way Out West, 1962
Oil on canvas
66 x 65 inches
Private collection

Untitled, 1963-64 (p. 104)
Oil on canvas
82 1/2 x 84 1/2 inches
Collection of Arne and Milly Glimcher,
New York

Untitled, 1963-64
Oil on canvas
82 1/2 x 84 1/2 inches
The Margulies Family Collection, Miami

Untitled, 1963-65
Oil on canvas on shaped wood veneer frame
82 1/2 x 84 1/2 inches
Walker Art Center, Minneapolis
Gift of the Albert A. List Family, 1972

Untitled, ca. 1964-66
Oil on canvas on shaped wood veneer frame
82 1/2 x 84 1/2 inches
Collection of the artist

Untitled, ca. 1964-66
Oil on canvas on shaped wood veneer frame
82 1/2 x 84 1/2 inches
Collection of Arne and Milly Glimcher,
New York

Untitled, ca. 1964-66
Oil on canvas
41 5/8 x 42 5/8 inches
The Museum of Contemporary Art, Los Angeles
Gift of Mr. and Mrs. Burton Tremaine

Untitled, ca. 1966-67 (p. 114)
Sprayed acrylic lacquer on shaped aluminum
60 inches diameter
Collection of the artist

Untitled, ca. 1966-67 (p. 115)
Sprayed acrylic lacquer on shaped aluminum
60 inches diameter
Collection of the artist

Untitled, 1967-68 (p. 117)
Acrylic lacquer on formed acrylic plastic
54 inches diameter
Norton Simon Museum, Pasadena
Fellows Acquisition Fund, 1969

Untitled, 1969
Acrylic lacquer on formed acrylic plastic
54 inches diameter
Collection of Arne and Milly Glimcher,
New York

Untitled, ca. 1970-71
Cast acrylic column
226 x 5 x 3 1/2 inches
Collection of the artist

Untitled, ca. 1970-71
Cast acrylic column
144 x 8 1/2 x 3 1/2 inches
Collection of the artist

Projects Documented
In the Exhibition

Slant Light Volume, 1971 (p. 125)
Walker Art Center, Minneapolis

Eye Level Wall Division, 1973 (p. 64)
The Pace Gallery, New York

Soft Wall, 1974 (p. 64)
The Pace Gallery, New York

Black Line Volume, 1975 (p. 122)
Museum of Contemporary Art, Chicago

Stairwell Slant Volume, 1976
University of Massachusetts, Amherst

Three Rooms, One Inside Another,
Scrim Division, Window, 1976
The Panza Collection
Varese, Italy

Scrim Veil—Black Rectangle—
Natural Light, 1977 (p. 67)
Whitney Museum of American Art, New York

Tilted Planes, proposed 1978
(unrealized) (pp.133, 135)
Oval Mall, Ohio State University, Columbus

Three-Plane Triangulation, 1979 (p. 123)
University Art Museum,
University of California, Berkeley

Aviary, proposed 1980 (unrealized)
Duncan Plaza, New Orleans

Filigreed Line, 1980 (pp. 138-39)
Wellesley College, Massachusetts

One Wall Removed, 1980
Malinda Wyatt Gallery, Venice, California

Portal Park Slice, 1980 (p. 70)
John W. Carpenter Park, Dallas

48 Shadow Planes, 1983 (pp. 120-21)
Old Post Office, Washington, D.C.

H.H.H. Memorial Plaza, proposed 1983
(unrealized) (p. 142)
Hubert Horatio Humphrey Center
University of Minnesota, Minneapolis

Nine Spaces, Nine Trees, 1983 (p. 140)
Public Safety Building Plaza, Seattle

Three Primary Forms, proposed 1983
(unrealized)
Battery Park City Commercial Plaza, New York

Two Running Violet V Forms, 1983 (pp. 71-72)
Stuart Collection
University of California, San Diego

Grand Avenue Viaduct, proposed 1985
(unrealized) (p 143)
Upper and lower Grand Avenues, Los Angeles

External Window, 1985 (p. 127)
The Pace Gallery, New York

A Single Plane: 324 Parts, 1985 (p. 141)
San Francisco Museum of Modern Art

Arts Enrichment Master Plan, proposed 1986
(unrealized) (pp. 150, 160-63, 166-68)
Miami International Airport

Scrim Hall, 1988 (p. 112)
(one of a series of transient campus markings)
Rice University, Houston

Three Project Sight Lines, proposed 1988
(unrealized) (p. 175)
Frank Lloyd Wright's "Fallingwater," Millrun,
Pennsylvania

Two Architectural Towers, proposed 1989
(unrealized) (pp. 146-47)
City Front Plaza, Chicago

Allée, proposed 1990 (unrealized) (p. 177)
Rhône-Alps, France

Pure Space, 1990 (p. 124)
The Museum of Contemporary Art, Los Angeles

Sentinel Plaza, 1990 (pp. 48-49, 144-45)
Pasadena Police Department

1 2 3 4°, 1992 (pp. 182-83, 186-87)
The Pace Gallery, New York

South Roundabout, proposed 1992 (pp. 156, 159)
Las Vegas

Installations

For each venue, the artist will create two works in the
spirit of light and space installations of the 1970s and
early 1980s, as well as a new installation determined
by the characteristics of each specific site.

Bibliography

Compiled by Sherri Schottlaender

Books about the artist and one-person exhibition catalogues

1987
Feinberg, Jean. *Perceiving the Garden: Robert Irwin at Wave Hill.* New York: Wave Hill, 1987.
Essay with brief overview of Irwin's work, as well as descriptions of his three installations at Wave Hill and their site-conditioned contexts.

1985
Being and Circumstance: Notes Toward a Conditional Art. Larkspur Landing, Calif.: The Lapis Press, in conjunction with The Pace Gallery and the San Francisco Museum of Modern Art, 1985.
Published in conjunction with exhibitions at The Pace Gallery, New York, and the San Francisco Museum of Modern Art, this book explicates Irwin's ideas about art and his work, and describes and illustrates seventeen projects.

1982
Irwin, Robert. "Set of Questions" in *American Artists on Art from 1940 to 1980*, ed. Ellen H. Johnson. New York: Harper & Row, 1982.
Placed in the section "Systemic and Conceptual Art," this is a reprint of a presentation given by Irwin at an international symposium on "Art Education at the Higher Level" held in Montreal in 1980.

Weschler, Lawrence. *Seeing is Forgetting the Name of the Thing One Sees: A Life of Contemporary Artist Robert Irwin.* Berkeley and Los Angeles: University of California Press, 1982.
Seminal book covers Irwin's life and work through 1981; much of the text is Irwin's own words.

1977
Robert Irwin. New York: Whitney Museum of American Art, 1977.
Essay "Notes Toward a Model" by Irwin outlines and explicates his ideas about art and his work.

1968
Robert Irwin. New York: The Jewish Museum, 1968.

Catalogue published simultaneously and in conjunction with exhibitions (and catalogues) of the work of Gene Davis and Richard Smith. Essay by John Coplans on Irwin describes his work's evolution from Abstract Expressionism to the acrylic discs.

Robert Irwin. Pasadena: Pasadena Art Museum, 1968.
Brochure accompanied exhibition, text by John Coplans: "Irwin completely rejects the traditional distinctions between the haptic and the optic which have served to separate painting and sculpture; he feels painting must be free to move in any direction."

Group exhibition catalogues and general monographs

1990
The Relationship Between Art and Architecture. Santa Monica: The Frederick R. Weisman Foundation, 1990.
Summary of a two-day workshop. Participants included: Daniel Buren, Germano Celant, John Chamberlain, Henry N. Cobb, Jean-Louis Cohen, Peter Eisenman, Mildred Friedman, Frank O. Gehry, Michael Graves, Henry T. Hopkins, Irwin, Donald Judd, Christopher Knight, Irving Lavin, Cesar Pelli, Michael Rotondi, Nancy Wexler, and Dr. Milton Wexler.

1984
Harris, Stacey Paleologos, ed. *Insights/On Sites: Perspective on Art in Public Places.* Washington, D.C.: Partners for Livable Places, 1984.
Five essays discuss different aspects of public art. Irwin's *Nine Spaces, Nine Trees* is discussed in Richard Andrew's essay "Artists and the Visual Definition of Cities: The Experience of Seattle."

1982
Form and Function: Proposals for Public Art for Philadelphia. Philadelphia: Pennsylvania Academy of the Fine Arts, 1982.
Essay by Penny Balkin Bach. Irwin's proposed project entitled *Philadelphia Stoop.* Artists included: Siah Armajani, Scott Burton, Dan Flavin, Richard Fleischner, Irwin, Sol LeWitt, and Martin Puryear, among others.

1981

Tuchman, Maurice. *Art in Los Angeles: Seventeen Artists in the Sixties.* Los Angeles: Los Angeles County Museum of Art, 1981.
Essay by Michele D. De Angelus, "Visually Haptic Space: The Twentieth-Century Luminism of Irwin and Bell." Author posits that the "haptic spaces" created by Irwin and Bell have their antecedents in the nineteenth-century art movement Luminism: "For the Luminists, as with Irwin and Bell, light was the vehicle chosen to effect . . . transubstantiation."

1980

Andre, Buren, Irwin, Nordman: Space as Support. Berkeley: University Art Museum, 1980.
Site-determined installations created by each artist specifically for the University Art Museum.
Essay "Space as Support" by curator Mark Rosenthal: "If Buren's work is a tour-de-force of logic, Robert Irwin's is a perceptual shock. . . . Neither subordinated by nor superior to the building, Irwin's artwork interacts with the Museum and is on equal footing with it."
Essay "Bonds between Art and Architecture" by Germano Celant explores philosophical underpinnings of Irwin's work

Poling, Clark V. *Contemporary Art in Southern California.* Atlanta: The High Museum of Art, 1980.
Exhibition included work by: Eleanor Antin, John Baldessari, Chris Burden, Ronald Davis, Charles Garabedian, Helen Mayer Harrison and Newton Harrison, Douglas Huebler, Irwin, Ed Moses, Bruce Nauman, Roland Reiss, and Edward Ruscha. Essay by Poling discusses each artist's work: "Like the subtle differentiations in one of Ad Reinhardt's all black paintings, the effect of Irwin's installations . . . is to focus the viewer on his own perceptual awareness and to foster an almost meditative condition."

1979

California Perceptions: Light and Space; Selections from the Wortz Collection. Fullerton, Calif.: California State University, Fullerton, Art Gallery, 1979.
Essay by Melinda Wortz. Artists included: Peter Alexander, Larry Bell, Vija Celmins, Ron Cooper, Tony de Lap, Laddie John Dill, Irwin, Craig

Kauffman, Peter Lodato, John McCracken, Eric Orr, Helen Pashgian, Hap Tivey, James Turrell, DeWain Valentine, and Douglas Wheeler.

1978

Weschler, Lawrence. (Text of brochure for "Robert Irwin" exhibition at University Art Museum, Berkeley; part of the museum's "Matrix" series). Berkeley: University Art Museum, 1978.
"His trajectory over the past twenty years has consisted of a complete transformation of intent and product: nothing could seem further from the work he was doing in 1958 than the work he does in 1978—and yet that transformation has been progressive and organic, a consistent series of responses to a sequence of unfolding questions, an unfurling self-dialogue."

1977

Painting and Sculpture in California: The Modern Era. San Francisco: San Francisco Museum of Modern Art, 1977.
Exhibition included three works by Irwin in the section "Color and Field Abstraction," which also included Larry Bell, Billy Al Bengston, Craig Kauffman, John McCracken, Kenneth Price, and others. "Robert Irwin's minimal line paintings of the early 1960's started him on an extended journey of extracting the essence of light and its colors . . . ."

1976

Critical Perspectives in American Art. Amherst, Mass.: Fine Arts Center Gallery, University of Massachusetts, Amherst, 1976.
Exhibition curated by Sam Hunter, Rosalind Krauss, and Marcia Tucker. Essay "Perceptual Fields," by Rosalind Krauss and Marcia Tucker, discusses the work of Irwin, Agnes Martin, and Richard Tuttle: "The import of this perceptual

Robert Irwin and his father, Los Angeles, early 1930s

theme within the course of such recent art . . . is
. . . that it uses the very act of seeing to express
a connection, or rather an absolute unity, between those things which earlier art had treated
dualistically."

The Last Time I Saw Ferus: 1957-1966.
Newport Beach, Calif.: Newport Harbor Art
Museum, 1976.
Essay by curator Betty Turnbull gives the history
of the Ferus Gallery.

Projects for PCA. Philadelphia: Pennsylvania
College of Fine Arts, 1976.
Artists included: Anne Healy, Patrick Ireland,
Irwin, and Charles Simonds. Essay by Janet
Kardon. (Description of Irwin's scrim installa-
tion): "This pure yet sensual work was unmeasur-
able, unknowable, unphotographable and
unforgettable."

1975
University of California, Irvine: 1965-75. La Jolla,
Calif.: La Jolla Museum of Contemporary Art,
1975. Catalogue for exhibition of the work of
artists who taught or studied at UC Irvine
between 1965 and 1975; emphasis on Irwin's
influence as a teacher.

A View Through. Long Beach, Calif.: The Art
Galleries, California State University, 1975.
Exhibition examining glass, plastic, and light as
used by Southern California artists; included the
work of Peter Alexander, Larry Bell and Dr.
Who?, Ron Cooper, Guy Dill, Laddie John Dill,
Doug Edge, Irwin, and Terry O'Shea.

1974
Illumination and Reflection. New York:
Whitney Museum of American Art, 1974.
Exhibition at the Whitney's Downtown Branch,
with Peter Alexander, Steven Antonakos,
Larry Bell, Hans Breder, Chryssa, Fred Eversley,
Dan Flavin, Irwin, Craig Kauffman, Leroy Lamis,
Stanley Landsman, Claudio Marzollo, Barbara
Mortimer, Louise Nevelson, Earl Reiback, Sylvia
Stone, Ruth Vollmer, and David Weinrib; each
artist contributed a statement to the publication.

Plagens, Peter. *Sunshine Muse: Contemporary Art on
the West Coast.* New York: Praeger, 1974.
Discusses Irwin's work in context of other West
Coast artists.

1973
American Art: Third Quarter Century. Seattle:
Contemporary Art Council of the Seattle Art
Museum, 1973.
Seventy-four artists represented a projected survey
of American art from 1970 forward. Catalogue
essayist Jan van der Marck says of Irwin's work:
"No artist has made painting more phenomenal
and color more sensorial. . . ."

Some Recent American Art. Melbourne, Australia:
The National Gallery of Victoria, 1973.
Exhibition organized by The International
Council of The Museum of Modern Art and
traveled to five Australian venues. Twenty-one
artists included Vito Acconci, Carl Andre,
John Baldessari, Dan Flavin, Irwin, Donald Judd,
Joseph Kosuth, Bruce Nauman, Robert Ryman,
and Richard Serra. Includes a statement by Irwin.

1972
USA: West Coast. Hamburg: Kunstverein in
Hamburg, 1972.
Exhibition included eighteen West Coast artists,
including Peter Alexander, Larry Bell, Billy Al
Bengston, Ron David, Irwin, Ed Moses, Kenneth
Price, and Edward Ruscha; traveled to three addi-
tional German venues. Essay by Helene Winer,
"The Los Angeles 'Look'," discusses briefly each
artist in the exhibition. She writes of Irwin's work:
"The scrim installations and columns are physical-
ly absolute while coming close to invisibility."

1971
Eleven Los Angeles Artists. London: The Arts
Council of Great Britain, 1971.
Exhibition at Hayward Gallery, with artists
John Altoon, Larry Bell, Richard Diebenkorn,
Newton Harrison, Maxwell Hendler, Irwin, John
McLaughlin, Bruce Nauman, Kenneth Price,
Edward Ruscha, and William Wegman. Short
essays by guest curators Maurice Tuchman and
Jane Livingston describe each artist's oeuvre and
place them in context with other L.A. artists.

A Report on the Art and Technology Program of the Los Angeles County Museum of Art 1967–71. Los Angeles: Los Angeles County Museum of Art, 1971.
Extensive documentation of the collaborations between artists and industry initiated by LACMA; report on Irwin's collaboration with artist James Turrell and Dr. Edward Wortz of the Garrett Corporation, and descriptions of their perceptual investigations.

Thirty-Second Biennial Exhibition of Contemporary American Painting. Washington, D.C.: The Corcoran Gallery of Art, 1971.
Exhibition included eleven "director's selections" (Richard Estes, Sam Francis, Irwin, Richard Jackson, Roy Lichtenstein, Frank Lobdell, David Novros, Philip Pearlstein, Edward Ruscha, Peter Saul, and David Stephens), those artists in turn chose eleven other artists for inclusion. Irwin created a site-specific work for the exhibition.

Transparency, Reflection, Light, Space: Four Artists; Peter Alexander, Larry Bell, Robert Irwin, Craig Kauffman. Los Angeles: UCLA Art Galleries, 1971.
Irwin interviewed by Frederick S. Wight, director of the UCLA Art Galleries.

Works for New Spaces. Minneapolis: Walker Art Center, 1970.
Twenty-two artists were commissioned to create new works for Walker Art Center's new facility; Irwin created a scrim installation.

1970
Larry Bell, Robert Irwin, Doug Wheeler. London: The Tate Gallery, 1970.
Essay by Michael Compton discussing the general characteristics of the "environmental" qualities of these three artists' work, and short overviews of each artist's oeuvre.

A Decade of California Color: 1960–1970. New York: The Pace Gallery, 1970
Exhibition included Peter Alexander, Charles Arnoldi, Larry Bell, Billy Al Bengston, Fred Eversley, Patrick Hogan, Irwin, Craig Kauffman, John McCracken, Edward Moses, Kenneth Price, Edward Ruscha, and DeWain Valentine.

Looking West 1970. Omaha, Nebr.: Joslyn Art Museum, 1970.
Group exhibition of California artists.

Permutations: Light and Color. Chicago: Museum of Contemporary Art, 1970.
Exhibition included the work of Los Angeles-area artists Peter Alexander, Chuck Arnoldi, Larry Bell, Ron Cooper, Mary Corse, Ron Davis, James DeFrance, Doug Edge, Fred Eversley, Irwin, Craig Kauffman, John McCracken, Terry O'Shea, Helen Pashgian, DeWain Valentine, and Norman Zammitt.

Sixty-Ninth American Exhibition. Chicago: Art Institute of Chicago, 1970.
Group exhibition included the work of twenty-one artists; Irwin represented by an acrylic disc.

1969
Robert Irwin—Doug Wheeler. Fort Worth, Tex.: Fort Worth Art Center Museum, 1969.
Essay by Jane Livingston, in which she discusses both artists' interests in light and perception: "[Irwin] emphasized verbally that what he required of the spectator was for him literally to 'enact the process of the work's conception'. . . ."

Kompass: West Coast USA. Eindhoven: Stedelijk van Abbemuseum, 1969.
Fourth in a series of exhibitions with the title "Kompass" organized by the van Abbemuseum beginning in 1961, exhibition concentrates on Los Angeles and San Francisco artists, including Larry Bell, Billy Al Bengston, Richard Diebenkorn, Irwin, Kenneth Price, Edward Kienholz, Bruce Nauman, and Edward Ruscha, among others.

West Coast 1945–1969. Pasadena: Pasadena Art Museum, 1969.
Exhibition included twenty-five Northern and Southern California artists. Text by John Coplans: "Irwin, Kauffman and Bell . . . uniquely focus upon a type of surface and color which is highly sensitive to direct, ambient and reflected light (or even the absence of light)."

1968
Late Fifties at the Ferus. Los Angeles: Los Angeles County Museum of Art, 1968.
Essay by James Monte.

Los Angeles Six. Vancouver:
The Vancouver Art Gallery, 1968.
Exhibition curated by John Coplans, included
Larry Bell, Ron Davis, Irwin, Craig Kauffman,
Edward Kienholz, and John McCracken.
Essay by Coplans: ". . . [Irwin] was the first
Southern California artist to break radically
the traditional format and to extend it beyond
the picture frame."

Untitled, 1968. San Francisco: San Francisco
Museum of Art, 1968.
Catalogue for national invitational exhibition
sponsored by the San Francisco Art Institute and
the San Francisco Museum of Art. Exhibition
included Joseph Cornell, Willem de Kooning,
Richard Diebenkorn, Irwin, Jasper Johns,
Roy Lichtenstein, Agnes Martin, Robert
Rauschenberg, Lucas Samaras, and others.

1966
Robert Irwin, Kenneth Price. Los Angeles:
Los Angeles County Museum of Art in conjunction
with the Museum's Contemporary Art Council,
and Lytton Gallery, 1966.
Essay on Irwin by Philip Leider discusses Irwin's
dot paintings.

1965
*Exhibition of the United States of America:
VIII Biennial of the Museum of Modern Art,
São Paulo, Brazil, 1965*. Pasadena:
Pasadena Art Museum, 1965.
Exhibition included work by Barnett Newman,
as well as Larry Bell, Billy Al Bengston, Irwin,
Donald Judd, Larry Poons, and Frank Stella.
Introduction by exhibition curator Walter Hopps:
"Ultimately, the work of all the artists in this exhi-
bition exists only to be experienced, not written
about, not confused with the ambiguity of words
or generalities the artists would reject."

The Responsive Eye. New York: The Museum of
Modern Art, 1965.
Essay by William Seitz.

1962
Fifty California Artists. New York: Whitney Museum
of American Art, 1962.

1960
Fifty Paintings by Thirty-Seven Painters.
Los Angeles: UCLA Art Galleries, 1960.
Exhibition organized by graduate student
Henry Hopkins for UCLA Art Gallery.

Periodicals

1993
Balken, Debra Bricker. "Robert Irwin at Pace."
Art in America 81, no. 1 (January 1993): 99.
"Unlike the austere and sometimes elusive projects
he has mounted in the past, this work was physi-
cally sumptuous as well as conceptually complex."

1992
Avgikos, Jan. (Review of *Untitled (1234°)* at
The Pace Gallery, New York.) *Artforum* 31,
no. 3 (November 1992): 103-104.
". . . he has managed a coup of sorts, articulating
his ideas in such a way that the meaning of contextual investigation and site-specificity is pliant, as
related to '70s formalism as to '80s commodity cri-
tiques and '90s social science."

Smith, Roberta. "Matter Turned Into Light and
Space." *The New York Times*, 25 September 1992,
section C, 29.
Review of installation at The Pace Gallery:
"The ultimate message of his work, simple yet profound, is the more you look, the more you see.
His success lies in the way he makes his own
visual explorations available to the viewer,
proving repeatedly that magic comprehended is no
less magical."

1991
Berman, Avis. "Public Sculpture's New Look."
Art News 90, no. 7 (September 1991): 102-109.
Discusses upsurge of interest in public art and site-
specific projects, as well as difficulties inherent in
such endeavors.

Krauss, Rosalind. "Overcoming the Limits of
Matter: On Revising Minimalism" in *Studies in
Modern Art* no. 1 (1991) (The Museum of Modern
Art), ed. James Leggio and Susan Weiley, pp.123-
41. Analysis of artists' search for "the perceptual
nothing, the visual sublime," with a lineage from

Albers to Reinhardt to Irwin, and how Irwin's work differed in intent from that of other Minimalists: "They were making objects; he was 'finding phenomena.'"

Wilson, William. "Pasadena Police Nab Robert Irwin." *Los Angeles Times*, 22 July 1991, section F, 1, 6-7.
Article discusses *Sentinel Plaza*, installed at police headquarters in Pasadena. Irwin: "You can't completely re-invent yourself for every project but I think the special thing artists bring to them is a willingness to involve themselves on an intimate qualitative level."

1990
"Plant Life" in "Goings on About Town," *The New Yorker*, 5 March 1990, 8.
Description of Irwin's project at 45th Street and Sixth and Seventh Avenues in Manhattan: ". . . startling and hilarious. The last thing you expect to find on 45th Street is neat suburban strips of evergreens growing a hundred feet in the air."

Joselit, David. "Public Art and the Public Purse." *Art in America* 78, no. 7 (July 1990): 143-50, 183.
Discusses various aspects of Dade County, Florida's "Art in Public Places" program, including Irwin's Miami International Airport project proposal.

1989
Joselit, David. "Lessons in Public Sculpture." *Art in America* 77, no. 12 (December 1989): 130-34.
Describes various works of art in the Stuart Collection (including Irwin's *Two Running Violet V Forms*), located on the campus of University of California, San Diego.

Lebowitz, Cathy, and Walter Robinson. "Artworld." *Art In America* 77, no. 9 (March 1989): 176.
Discusses the Weisman Foundation-sponsored panel "Art and Architecture," with participants Germano Celant, John Chamberlain, Peter Eisenman, Frank Gehry, Michael Graves, Irwin, Donald Judd, Cesar Pelli, and others.

Morgan, Stuart. "Past, Present, Future." *Artscribe*, no. 76: 53-56.
Interview with Count Giuseppe Panza di Biumo, who calls Irwin "an exemplary Los Angeles artist."

1988
Freudenheim, Susan. "Under the Singing Eucalyptus Tree . . ." *Artforum* 26, no. 8 (April 1988): 124-29.
Discusses the Stuart Collection.

1987
Brenson, Michael. "City as Sculpture Garden: Seeing the New and Daring." *The New York Times*, 17 July 1987, C1, 30.
Discussion of public sculpture in and around Manhattan, including Irwin's installations at Wave Hill, in the Bronx.

Goodman, Jonathan. "Perceiving the Garden: Robert Irwin at Wave Hill." *Arts Magazine* 62, no. 3 (November 1987): 30-32.
Review of Irwin's three projects realized at Wave Hill, describing how each interacts with a different aspect of the surrounding environment.

Phillips, Patricia C. "Robert Irwin: Wave Hill." *Artforum* 26, no. 3 (November 1987): 134-35.
Brief review of installations at Wave Hill.

1986
Boettger, Suzaan. "Robert Irwin: The Pace Gallery." *Artforum* 24, no. 5 (January 1986): 87.
Review of exhibition of documentation of fourteen site-specific installations from 1977 to 1985, eight realized, six not.

Esterow, Milton. "How Public Art Becomes a Political Hot Potato." *Art News* 85, no. 1 (January 1986): 75-79.
Includes a conversation with Irwin about his work, both built and unbuilt.

McGill, Douglas C. "Sculpture Goes Public." *The New York Times Magazine*, 27 April 1986, 42-45, 63, 66-67, 85, 87.
Discussion of public art projects, including the Washington Post Office project in Washington, D.C.

Princenthal, Nancy. "Robert Irwin at Pace."
Art in America 74, no. 4 (April 1986): 193-94.
Brief review: "Both of these installations . . .
achieved the almost sublime resonance that
distinguishes Irwin's most effective pieces."

1985
Adcock, Craig. "Perceptual Edges: The
Psychology of James Turrell's Light and Space."
Arts Magazine 59, no. 6 (February 1985): 124-28.
Discussion of James Turrell's work, with extensive
attention to his collaborations with Irwin and
Dr. Edward Wortz on the "Art and Technology"
program at the Los Angeles County Museum
of Art in the late 1960s.

Atkins, Robert. "Robert Irwin." *Arts Magazine*
60, no. 4 (December 1985): 102.
Brief review of exhibition at The Pace Gallery,
New York.

Tomkins, Calvin. "The Art World: Knowing in
Action." *The New Yorker*, 11 November 1985,
144-49.
Tomkins juxtaposes a review of The Museum
of Modern Art exhibition "Contrasts of Form:
Geometric Abstract Art 1910-1980" with a discus-
sion of the metaphysical and abstract aspects of
Irwin's work.

Weschler, Lawrence. "Seeing." *The New Yorker*,
30 September 1985, 27-29.
Conversation with the artist on the occasion
of his exhibition at The Pace Gallery.

1984
McEvilley, Thomas. "Robert Irwin:
Public Safety Building Plaza, Old Post Office."
Artforum 22, no. 10 (Summer 1984): 96.
Description and critique of Irwin's *Nine Spaces,
Nine Trees* in Seattle, and the installation at the
Old Post Office in Washington, D.C.

1983
Failing, Patricia. "MOCA." *Art News* 82, no. 8
(October 1983): 105-109.
Article about the opening of The Museum of
Contemporary Art, Los Angeles, and Irwin's
vision as a founding trustee.

_____. "Big Bird on Campus." *Art News* 82,
no. 9 (November 1983): 132, 135.
Discussion of the Stuart Collection at the
University of California, San Diego.

Tomkins, Calvin. "Like Water in a Glass."
The New Yorker, 21 March 1983, 92-97.
Article about interactions between art and architecture: "According to Irwin, public art provides
the context for the necessary redefinition of
art in our time."

Wortz, Melinda. "Robert Irwin: University of
California." *Artforum* 22, no. 2 (October 1983):
81-82.
Discussion of the Stuart Collection.

1982
"Down the Granite Path." *Art News* 81, no. 1
(January 1982): 16, 20.
Description of Irwin's Cor-ten steel sculpture in
Carpenter Plaza in downtown Dallas, and the
problems he encountered in realizing it.

Butterfield, Jan. "New Light on a Socratic Artist."
San Francisco Chronicle Book Review, 4 April 1982, 3.
Review of *Seeing is Forgetting the Name of the Thing
One Sees*, by Lawrence Weschler.

Schjeldahl, Peter. "Improvising in Art and Life."
The New York Times Book Review, 18 April 1982,
3, 30.
Review of *Seeing is Forgetting the Name of the Thing
One Sees*.

Singerman, Howard. (Review of "Art in Los
Angeles: Seventeen Artists in the Sixties" at
the Los Angeles County Museum of Art.)
Artforum 20, no. 7 (March 1982): 75-77.
Review noting Irwin's inclusion in both sections of
the exhibition, "Seventeen Artists in the Sixties,"
and "The Museum as Site."

Weschler, Lawrence. "Lines of Inquiry." *Art in
America* 70, no. 3 (March 1982): 102-109.
Excerpt from *Seeing is Forgetting the Name
of the Thing One Sees*.

_____. "Taking Art to Point Zero—I." *The New
Yorker*, 8 March 1982, 48-94; and "Taking Art to
Point Zero—II," 15 March 1982, 52-105.

In-depth two part article discussing Irwin and his work, with extensive quotes from the artist; article excerpted from *Seeing is Forgetting the Name of the Thing One Sees*.

1981
Butterfield, Jan. "The Enigma Suffices: Robert Irwin, Room with Twin Skylights." *Images & Issues* 1, no. 3 (Winter 1980-81): 38-40.
Description of the changing experience of visiting Irwin's installation at Malinda Wyatt Gallery, Venice, California, at different times of the day.

Stevens, Mark. "California Dreamers."
Newsweek, 17 August 1981, 78-79.
Review of the Los Angeles County Museum of Art exhibition "Seventeen Artists in the Sixties."

Wortz, Melinda. "Surrendering to Presence: Robert Irwin's Esthetic Integration."
Artforum 20, no. 3 (November 1981): 63-68.
Overview of Irwin's site-determined work, including work at Wellesley, Dallas's Carpenter Plaza, and the University Art Museum at University of California, Berkeley.

1979
Albright, Thomas. "San Francisco: Primarily Biological." *Art News* 78, no. 6 (Summer 1979): 156-57.
Review of installations at the University Art Museum, Berkeley; writer feels that the building's architectural Brutalism overwhelmed both Irwin's and Daniel Buren's installations.

Atkins, Robert. "Irwin Trips the Light Fantastic."
Artweek 10, no. 15 (April 14, 1979): 1, 16.
Review of Berkeley installation.

Fischer, Hal. (Review of "Andre, Buren, Irwin, Nordman: Space as Support" at University Art Museum, Berkeley.) *Artforum* 18, no. 2 (October 1979): 64-66.
Irwin's installation described as more "extreme" than his previous work; exhibition also included installations by Carl Andre, Daniel Buren, and Maria Nordman.

Knight, Christopher. "Robert Irwin: San Diego State University Art Gallery." *Artforum* 18, no. 2 (October 1979): 77-78.
Brief review of scrim installation.

Robert Irwin and friend, Los Angeles, 1940s

Plagens, Peter. "Robert Irwin's Bar Paintings."
Artforum 17, no. 7 (March 1979): 41-43.
Analysis of Irwin's "bar paintings," and their importance within his oeuvre; review of "Matrix" series exhibition of his work at the University Art Museum, Berkeley.

Wolfe, Claire. "On Art Writing: Part One, Structuring the Conceptual Environment." *Journal* (Los Angeles), no. 23 (June-July 1979): 44-46.
Discussion of the absence of effective critical art writing and its impact on artists working in Los Angeles in the seventies.

1978
Art Actuel: Skira Annual (Switzerland), no. 4 (1978).
Theme of the annual is "The Subjects of Contemporary Art." Irwin's work included in the section "The Image of Nature." Statement by Irwin: "While there is no one transcending 'Art,' there is one infinite subject: The subject of art is aesthetic perception."

1977
Albright, Thomas. "Robert Irwin: 'Everything I've Done in the Last Five Years Doesn't Exist'."
Art News 76, no. 6 (Summer 1977): 49-54.
Traces development of Irwin's work, up through the work included in the 1977 Whitney Museum of American Art one-person exhibition.

Butterfield, Jan. "Made in California." *American Art Review* 4, no. 1 (July 1977): 118-44.
Review of exhibition "Painting and Sculpture in California: The Modern Era," with over 300 works by 200 artists; Irwin included under the heading "Color and Field."

Herrera, Hayden. "Manhattan Seven." *Art in America* 65, no. 4 (July-August 1977): 50-63. Article discusses seven artists' (Red Grooms, Hans Haacke, Irwin, Gordon Matta-Clark, Charles Simonds, Alan Sonfist, and Stephen Varble) specific works "that intimately engage New York City either as site, subject, material, or all three." Irwin's *Black Planes—Shadows, Park Avenue* and *Line Rectangle, World Trade Center*, installed for the Whitney exhibition, are discussed.

Kramer, Hilton. "A Career That Rejected Studio Art." *The New York Times*, 8 May 1977, D25. Review of Whitney exhibition: "This is, after all, Mr. Irwin's idea of paradise, not ours, and we are glad to leave it to him."

Levine, Edward. "Robert Irwin's Recent Work." *Artforum* 16, no. 4 (December 1977): 24-29. Overview of Irwin's work, including the Whitney installations, as well as a general discussion of Irwin's ideas.

Ratcliff, Carter. "New York Letter." *Art International* 21, no. 4 (July-August 1977): 73-77. Review of Whitney exhibition.

Russell, John. "Art: Robert Irwin at the Whitney." *The New York Times*, 22 April 1977, C21. Brief review.

Schwartz, Ellen. "'Floating' a Line in Space." *Art News* 76, no. 6 (Summer 1977): 52-53. Review of Whitney exhibition, suggesting parallels between Irwin's work and that of Manet and Magritte.

Weschler, Lawrence. "Robert Irwin's Alchemy of Perception." *The Village Voice*, 9 May 1977, 79. Review of Whitney exhibition, with some discussion of Irwin's earlier work.

"Robert Irwin's Whitney Project—Retrospects and Prospects." *Journal* (Los Angeles), no. 15 (July-August 1977): 14-23. Overview of Irwin's career, discussing his early work and his various artistic evolutions.

1976

Butterfield, Jan. "Robert Irwin: On the Periphery of Knowing." *Arts Magazine* 50, no. 6 (February 1976): 72-77. Interview with Irwin, who discusses his ideas about art and perception.

Hazlitt, Gordon J. "'An Incredibly Beautiful Quandary'." *Art News* 75, no. 5 (May 1976): 36-38. Title of article is quote from Irwin, who, along with other artists, discusses "the state of art" in the mid-seventies.

Levine, Edward. "Robert Irwin: World Without Frame." *Arts Magazine* 50, no. 6 (February 1976): 72-77. Review of exhibition at the Museum of Contemporary Art, Chicago.

Marmer, Nancy. (Review of work at Mizuno Gallery, Los Angeles.) *Artforum* 14, no. 6 (February 1976): 69-70. Description of experiential qualities of Irwin's installation.

Morrison, C. L. (Review of exhibition at the Museum of Contemporary Art, Chicago.) *Artforum* 14, no. 6 (February 1976): 67. Review of two installations: "Irwin's work is a fascinating contrast to objects. . . . But Irwin's enormously sophisticated illusions can create a 'beautiful altogether,' precisely as a foil to the dross around us."

Perlmutter, Elizabeth. "A Hotbed of Advanced Art." *Art News* 75, no. 1 (January 1976): 44-46. Review of exhibition "University of California, Irvine: 1965-75," organized by Melinda Wortz. Description of Irwin scrim installation: "The space is silent and empty; the viewer by necessity remains outside, looking in."

Smith, Roberta. "Robert Irwin: The Subject is Sight." *Art in America* 64, no. 2 (March-April 1976): 68-73. Discussion of exhibition at the Museum of Contemporary Art, Chicago, and of the evolution of Irwin's work from Abstract Expressionist-influenced paintings to scrim pieces.

Wortz, Melinda. "Self-Scrutiny and Scrims."
Art News 75, no. 1 (January 1976): 64-66.
Brief review of Mizuno Gallery installation.

1975
David, Douglas. "The Searcher." *Newsweek*,
29 December 1975, 53.
Discussion of Irwin's ideas about art, and specific
descriptions of his "volumes" installed at the Fort
Worth Art Museum.

Dreiss, Joseph. (Review of exhibition at The Pace
Gallery, New York.) *Arts Magazine* 49, no. 6
(February 1975): 16.
Brief review.

Nordland, Gerald. "Los Angeles Newsletter."
Art International 19, no. 10 (December 20, 1975):
29-31.
Review of "A View Through" at California State
University, Long Beach, group exhibition of
artists using transparent materials.

Rosing, Larry. (Review of exhibition at The Pace
Gallery, New York.) *Art in America* 63, no. 2
(March-April 1975): 87.
Brief review.

1974
Butterfield, Jan. "An Uncompromising Other
Way." *Arts Magazine* 48, no. 9 (June 1974): 52-55.
Article about Irwin's work, specifically 1974 Pace
Gallery installation and 1974 Mizuno Gallery
installation; author questions whether or not
Irwin's work obviates the act of criticism.

Leopold, Michael. "Los Angeles." *Art International*
18, no. 6 (Summer 1974): 38-39, 63.
Review of installation at Mizuno Gallery, Los
Angeles.

Matos, José. (Review of exhibition at The Pace
Gallery, New York.) *Artforum* 12, no. 6 (February
1974): 78.
Brief review.

Montgomery, Cara. "West Coast Report."
Arts Magazine 47, no. 6 (April 1973): 71-72.
Review of the exhibition "Works In Space" at the
San Francisco Museum of Art, which included
Stephen Antonokos, Ronald Bladen, Sam Gilliam,

Irwin, and Dorothea Rockburne; describes
Irwin's installation.

Moore, Alan. (Review of installation at the
Museum of Contemporary Art, Chicago.)
Artforum 12, no. 8 (April 1974): 67.
Brief review.

"Museum News." *Art Journal* 32, no. 3
(Spring 1973): 319-24.
Review of exhibition of Irwin's work at the
Museum of Art, Rhode Island School of Design.
Described as a "mini-retrospective," exhibition
consisted of nine works: "For several days during
the show, Irwin was 'in residence'. . . and his
conversation itself is a work of art!"

Plagens, Peter. (Review of *Portal*, installed at
Mizuno Gallery, Los Angeles.) *Artforum* 12, no. 8
(April 1974): 83-84.
Brief review.

Stitelman, Paul. "Robert Irwin." *Arts Magazine* 48,
no. 5 (February 1974): 65.
Brief review of exhibition at The Pace Gallery.

Terbell, Melinda. "African Art in Motion."
Art News 73, no. 3 (March 1974): 75-76.
Article reviews three exhibitions in Los Angeles,
including Irwin at Mizuno Gallery.

1972
Butterfield, Jan. "The State of the Real: Robert
Irwin Discusses the Activities of an Extended
Consciousness—Part I." *Arts Magazine* 46, no. 9
(Summer 1972): 47-49; "Robert Irwin: 'Re-shaping
the Shape of Things'—Part 2, The Myth of the
Artist." *Arts Magazine* 47, no. 1 (September-
October, 1972): 30-32.
Two-part article is a compilation of tapes of
Irwin's lectures and conversations with the author;
he explains the progression of his work from
Abstract Expressionist canvases to his "volumes."

Mackintosh, Alastair. "Robert Irwin: An Interview
with Alastair Mackintosh." *Art and Artists* 6, no.
12 (March 1972): 24-27.
Irwin explains his decision not to allow photography of his work, and his move away from making
objects toward dealing directly with perception.

1971

Baker, Elizabeth C. "Los Angeles, 1971."
Art News 70, no. 5 (September 1971): 27-39.
Overview of the state of art in Los Angeles in
1971, the lack of criticism and museum support.

Drath, Viola Herms. "The 32nd Corcoran
Biennial: Art as Visual Event." *Art International* 15,
no. 5 (May 20, 1971): 40-44.
Review of the Corcoran Gallery of Art's "32nd
Biennial of American Painting"; brief critique
of Irwin's scrim piece installed in the building's
rotunda.

Miller, Donald. "Washington." *Arts Magazine* 45,
no. 6 (April 1971): 76-77.
Review of the Corcoran Biennial: "The most
impressive work in the show was not a painting.
It was Irwin's serene environment created for the
Corcoran rotunda. . . . The artist clearly succeed-
ed with his purpose of heightening perceptual
experience within a given or existing space-
light situation."

Plagens, Peter. (Review of "Transparency,
Reflection, Light, Space: Four Artists" at
University of California, Los Angeles.)
Artforum 9, no. 7 (March 1971): 68-69.
Review states: "Irwin's stairwell is by far the most
ambitious work because in this crowd it is the
least material . . . and takes the most chances."

Siegel, Jeanne. (Review of exhibition at
The Pace Gallery, New York.) *Art News* 70, no. 4
(Summer 1971): 14.
Review of acrylic resin column installation;
reviewer feels they are less successful than Irwin's
discs because they "sacrifice the contemplative,
almost mystical experience of the discs. . . ."

Terbell, Melinda. "Los Angeles." *Arts Magazine*
45, no. 5 (March 1971): 47-48.
Review of "Transparency, Reflection, Light,
Space: Four Artists," with description of Irwin's
stairwell installation: "As with all of Irwin's work,
and the other works in the show, the more time
invested in the experience, the greater are the
perceptual rewards."

1970

Compton, Michael. "Controlled Environment:
Larry Bell, Robert Irwin and Doug Wheeler at
the Tate Gallery." *Art and Artists* 5, no. 2
(May 1970): 45.
Discussion of these three artists' work: "Not only
is their work constructed to operate at a consciously perceptual level but it is devoid of
obvious talking points. . . ."

_____."UK Commentary." *Studio International* 179,
no. 923 (June 1970): 269-70.
Review of Bell, Irwin, Wheeler exhibition at
the Tate Gallery: "Prolonged contemplation
of the disc could produce very different sensation
from a shorter look: notably an even more complete dematerialization of the objects including
the wall surfaces."

Plagens, Peter. (Review of installation at the
artist's studio.) *Artforum* 9, no. 4 (December
1970): 88-89.
Review of acrylic resin columns; feels that they
will never be more than "optically interesting."

Roberts, Keith. "Leeds and London." *Burlington
Magazine* 112, no. 807 (June 1970): 415-16.
Review of Tate Gallery exhibition.

Russell, David. "London." *Arts Magazine* 44,
no. 8 (Summer 1970): 53.
Brief review of Tate Gallery exhibition.

Sharp, Willoughby. "New Directions in Southern
California Sculpture." *Arts Magazine* 44, no. 8
(Summer 1970): 35-38.
Overview of the work of L.A. artists, including
Michael Asher, Larry Bell, Billy Al Bengston,
Irwin, Craig Kauffman, John McCracken,
Eric Orr, James Turrell, and others.

Terbell, Melinda. "Los Angeles." *Arts Magazine*
45, no. 2 (November 1970): 53.
Review of installation of acrylic columns at artist's
studio; reviewer calls these works Irwin's "first
sculptures."

Wilson, William. "A Look Back at the Ferus."
Los Angeles Times, 25 November 1968, section
IV, 12.

Review of exhibition "Late Fifties at the Ferus" at Los Angeles County Museum of Art; reviewer says that Irwin's Pick-up Sticks paintings set the tone for the "light and forward movement."

1969
Ashton, Dore. "New York Commentary." *Studio International* 178, no. 917 (December 1969): 230-31.
Brief review of discs at The Pace Gallery, New York.

Bengston, Billy Al. "Late Fifties at the Ferus: A Participant Refuses to Take the Show Lying Down." *Artforum* 7, no. 5 (January 1969): 33-35.
Idiosyncratic review lists nineteen artists and evaluates whether or not the work included in the exhibition "fits" the time period covered.

Krauss, Rosalind. (Review of exhibition at The Pace Gallery, New York.) *Artforum* 8, no. 4 (December 1969): 70.
Review of acrylic discs; author finds them "both thoughtless and effete."

Kurtz, Stephen A. (Review of exhibition at The Pace Gallery, New York.) *Art News* 68, no. 7 (November 1969): 19c.
Review of "translucent plastic" discs; author terms them "Irwin's most successful illusionistic experiment."

Ratcliff, Carter. "New York." *Art International* 13, no. 10 (Christmas 1969): 71-75.
Review of installations at The Museum of Modern Art and at The Pace Gallery.

Seldis, Henry J. "Pasadena's Lopsided West Coast Survey." *Los Angeles Times Calendar*, 30 November 1969, 78.
Review of "West Coast: 1945-1969" at Pasadena Art Museum, curated by John Coplans; reviewer feels that curator omitted key artists, but that there were "important" works to be seen by Larry Bell, Irwin, Craig Kauffman, and others.

Selz, Peter, with Jane Livingston. "Two Generations in L.A.: West Coast Report." *Art in America* 57, no. 1 (January-February 1969): 92-97.

Overview of "generations" of Los Angeles artists, with Irwin falling into the "first generation" (with Billy Al Bengston, Ed Kienholz, Kenneth Price, and others): "It is tempting to place [Ron Cooper] categorically alongside light artists James Turrell and Doug Wheeler, loosely subsuming all three under the pervasive influence of Bob Irwin."

Stiles, Knute. "'Untitled, 68': The San Francisco Annual Becomes an Invitational." *Artforum* 7, no. 5 (January 1969): 50-52.
Review of exhibition.

1968
Baker, Elizabeth C. (Review of exhibition at The Pace Gallery, New York.) *Art News* 67, no. 3 (May 1968): 15-16.
Brief review of discs; writer states ". . . the whole idea seems a bit overproduced. However this is the most interesting work Irwin has done. . . ."

Feldman, Anita. "Gene Davis, Robert Irwin, Richard Smith." *Arts Magazine* 42, no. 7 (May 1968): 54.
Review of three one-person exhibitions at the Jewish Museum, New York.

"Light on Light." *Time*, 10 May 1968, 68.
In context of exhibition at the Jewish Museum, writer quotes Irwin: "'What you finally have is no beginning and no end, but a series of physical experiences moving on to the infinite.'"

Livingston, Jane. (Letter to the editors of *Artforum*.) *Artforum* 7, no. 1 (September 1968): 6.
Letter takes issue with Emily Wasserman's May 1968 review of Irwin's works at the Jewish Museum, especially her use of adjectives "staged," and "theatrical," and with the magazine's reproduction of *Untitled* (1966-67) [aluminum disc] on the cover. Includes rebuttal by Emily Wasserman.

Perrault, John. "Out of the Doldrums." *The Village Voice*, 28 March 1968, 18, 20.
Review of Jewish Museum exhibitions of Irwin, Davis, and Smith: "These mysterious 'mandalas' approach that unfashionable and rather vague category known as the sublime."

"Place in the Sun." *Time*, 30 August 1968, 38-41.
Discussion of flourishing Southern California art,
calling Irwin "something of a guru" to group of
young artists.

Robins, Corinne. "The Circle in Orbit." *Art in
America* 56, no. 6 (November-December 1968):
62-65.
Discussion of the circle as a part of artistic vocabulary; Irwin's discs included as part of an artistic
tradition.

Seldis, Henry J. "A Broad but Rare Contemporary
View." *Los Angeles Times Calendar*, 17 November
1968, 56.
Review of "Untitled, 1968" at San Francisco
Museum of Modern Art; mentions Irwin's disc as
being "intriguing."

Simon, Rita. (Review of exhibition at The Pace
Gallery, New York.) *Arts Magazine* 42, no. 7
(May 1968): 64.
Brief review of discs.

Terbell, Melinda. "Robert Irwin." *Arts Magazine*
42, no. 6 (April 1968): 55.
Review of exhibition at Pasadena Art Museum.

_____. (Review of "Los Angeles 6" at Vancouver
Art Gallery.) *Arts Magazine* 42, no. 7 (May
1968): 61.
Review of exhibition organized by John Coplans
that included Irwin's discs, as well as work by
Larry Bell, Gene Davis, Craig Kauffman,
Edward Kienholz, and John McCracken.

Wasserman, Emily. "Robert Irwin, Gene Davis,
Richard Smith: The Jewish Museum Mounts a
Hard-to-Assess 3-Man Show." *Artforum* 6, no. 9
(May 1968): 47-49.
Review of exhibition; reviewer likes the work
but questions the "theatrical" presentation.

Wilson, William. "Robert Irwin's Works at
Pasadena Museum." *Los Angeles Times*, 19 January
1968, section 4, 3.
Brief review of discs.

1967
Coplans, John. "L.A. Art Bloom." *Vogue* 150, no.
8 (November 1, 1967): 184-87, 232-33.
Discussion of Larry Bell, Billy Al Bengston, Ron
Davis, Irwin, Craig Kauffman, Ed Kienholz, John
Mason, John McCracken, Kenneth Price, and
Peter Voulkos. "Perhaps no artist is more responsible than Robert Irwin for injecting a rigorous
professionalism into the milieu. Irwin's visionary
obsessiveness has had a powerful effect on
younger artists."

Kozloff, Max. (Review of exhibition at The Pace
Gallery, New York.) *Artforum* 5, no. 5
(January 1967): 56.
Review of dot paintings: ". . . one feels in the pres-
ence of a personality who may be partly a monk,
and partly a physicist, but is above all, an artist."

Lippard, Lucy R. "The Silent Art." *Art in America*
55, no. 1 (January-February 1967): 58-63.
Main content of article is about Ad Reinhardt and
Yves Klein, but younger artists' "monotonal" work
is discussed, including paragraph about Irwin's
dot paintings.

Livingston, Jane. (Review of exhibition at Irving
Blum Gallery, New York.) *Artforum* 6, no. 4
(December 1967): 62.
Group exhibition: Flavin, Irwin, Judd, Kauffman,
and Stella; reviewer laments lack of new Irwin
work being exhibited in Los Angeles.

Waldman, Diane. (Review of exhibition at
The Pace Gallery, New York.) *Art News* 65, no. 9
(January 1967): 14.
Brief review of dot paintings: "The four paintings
. . . represent a continuous reduction and clarifica-
tion of means; the result is a complex statement
asserting itself with quiet authority."

Wilson, William. "The Explosion that Never
Went Boom." *Saturday Review*, 23 September
1967, 54-56.
General discussion about California art and different "movements"—the Ferus group, "finish
fetish," the work of Conner, Diebenkorn, Foulkes,
Goode, Ruscha: "Robert Irwin has yet to be fully
credited for his exquisite experiments suggesting
that his pale aurora borealis of color exists off and
in front of the surface of the painting."

1966

Hudson, Andrew. "Letter from Washington." *Art International* 10, no. 6 (Summer 1966): 130-31. Review of the VIII São Paulo Biennial on view at the National Collection of Fine Arts in Washington, D.C.

Ives, Colta Feller. (Review of exhibition at The Pace Gallery, New York.) *Arts Magazine* 41, no. 3 (December 1966-January 1967): 72. Brief review of dot paintings: "Outside of their technical perfectionism, Mr. Irwin's canvases also serve to emphasize how very far we've come from Pointillism."

Kozloff, Max. "São Paulo in Washington." *The Nation* 202, no. 9 (February 28, 1966): 250-52. Review of São Paulo Biennial on view in Washington: "By far the most delicate and radical of the Los Angeles artists is Robert Irwin."

Kramer, Hilton. "U.S. Art From São Paulo on View in Washington." *The New York Times*, 29 January 1966), 22. Review consists mainly of criticism of curator Water Hopps' criteria for choice of artists included.

Leider, Philip. "The Best of the Lack-Lustre." *The New York Times*, 7 August 1966, 14D. Review of "Robert Irwin/Kenneth Price" exhibition at Los Angeles County Museum of Art, with Irwin's dot paintings exhibited: "It is in their challenge to the prevailing dedication to the 'logic of the picture plane' that the importance of these new paintings will be measured."

Rose, Barbara. "Los Angeles: The Second City." *Art in America* 54, no. 1 (January-February 1966): 110-15. Overview of art in L.A., mentioning Irwin's "painstaking" integrity, and his influence on younger artists such as Larry Bell and Billy Al Bengston.

Wilson, William. "Couple of Bogey Men Add Luster to an Art Tradition." *Los Angeles Times*, 11 July 1966, section 4, 10. Review of Irwin/Price exhibition at LACMA.

Of Irwin's work: "They are remarkably homogenized, but the result of all this tough guy craft is a total sensation of tremulous lyricism."

1965

Coplans, John. "Los Angeles: The Scene." *Art News* 64, no. 1 (March 1965): 28-29, 56-58. Discussion of the emergence in Los Angeles of different sort of art than that in San Francisco: ". . . Edward Kienholz, Robert Irwin and Craig Kauffman, were to constitute the foundations of what was to lead to the development of the most adventurous painting and sculpture in Southern California."

_____. "The New Abstraction on the West Coast, U.S.A." *Studio International* 169, no. 865 (May 1965): 192-200. Overview of "abstraction" as practiced by Los Angeles and San Francisco artists; cites Irwin's line paintings.

Irwin, Robert. (Statement.) *Artforum* 3, no. 9 (June 1965): 23. Statement concerning photographic reproductions of his work. ". . . why do we insist on the language of duality by reproductions, negating the essential truth of the painting? And the answer can only be: expediency."

1964

Ashton, Dore. (Review of "Seven New Artists" at Sidney Janis Gallery, New York). *Arts & Architecture* 81, no. 6 (June 1964): 8-9, 33. "The passivity of these canvases more or less typifies the branch of the esthetic movement in which totally non-committal effects are sought."

Coplans, John. "Circle of Styles on the West Coast." *Art in America* 52, no. 3 (June 1964): 24-41. Overview of San Francisco and L.A. art: "Irwin is a visionary with the most intense moral fervor which gives him an enormous sense of excitement about being an artist here and now. This is backed by an acute sense of vision that becomes a visionary obsessiveness. . . ."

Fried, Michael. "New York Letter." *Art International* 8, no. 5-6 (Summer 1964): 82. Review of "Seven New Artists: ". . . provided little of interest apart from five paintings by the California painter Robert Irwin."

Leider, Philip. "The Cool School." *Artforum* 2, no. 12 (Summer 1964): 47. Discussion of the "avant-garde" disposing of the "weary, stale, flat and unprofitable" in art; Irwin's line paintings ". . . supply an extraordinary quality of tension to the canvas by a perfect minimum of means . . ."

Tillim, Sidney. (Review of "Seven New Artists" at Sidney Janis Gallery, New York.) *Arts Magazine* 38, no. 10 (September 1964): 62-63. Brief review. Exhibition included Arakawa, Larry Bell, Charles Hinman, Irwin (line paintings), Norman Ives, Robert Slutsky, and Robert Whitman: "The color is tonal and the effect is of a capricious austerity."

1963
van der Marck, Jan. "The Californians." *Art International* 7, no. 5 (May 1963): 28-31. Review of "Fifty California Artists," exhibition organized by the San Francisco Museum of Art; Irwin called a practitioner of "purist painting."

1962
Bogat, Regina. "Fifty California Artists." *Artforum* 1, no. 7 (January 1962): 23-25. Review of exhibition at the San Francisco Museum of Art: "The way subjective feeling can be expressed with an extreme limitation of means is explored by Robert Irwin, Art Holman, Leslie Kerr, and David Simpson, who show the life present in metaphysical painting on the West Coast."

1959
Langsner, Jules. "Cremean, Gottlieb, Irwin." *Art News* 58, no. 5 (Summer 1959): 60. Brief review of Irwin's Abstract Expressionist works: "Irwin paints with a sense of exhilaration in the way color and texture can be sprung into an independent mode of existence."

Photo Credits

The following list, keyed to page numbers, applies to photographs for which a separate acknowledgment is due.

Title page: Joel Meyerowitz, courtesy of *The New Yorker*. 18 (top): © Réunion des musées nationaux; (bottom) © 1993 The Museum of Modern Art, New York. 19: © 1993 Willem de Kooning / ARS, New York; © 1983 by The Metropolitan Museum of Art, New York. 48-49: Philipp Scholz Rittermann. 52: Courtesy of Paula Cooper Gallery, New York. 54: © 1993 Douglas M. Parker. 64: Paula Goldman. 67: Richard Marshall. 70 (top): Tom Fox. 71 (top), 72: Philipp Scholz Rittermann. 71 (bottom): Joan Tewkesbury. 76, 80-84, 86-87: © 1993 Douglas M. Parker. 88: William Claxton. 92: Patricia Faure. 98: © 1993 Douglas M. Parker. 100: Bill Jacobson Studio, courtesy of The Pace Gallery, New York. 101-102: © 1993 Douglas M. Parker. 104: Bill Jacobson Studio, courtesy of The Pace Gallery, New York. 105, 107-108: © 1993 Douglas M. Parker. 110: Dennis Hopper. 112: Paul Hester. 114-17: © 1993 Douglas M. Parker. 120-21: Don Thalacker, John Tennant. 123: Colin McRae. 124: Paula Goldman. 126: Bill Jacobson Studio, courtesy of The Pace Gallery, New York. 133, 135, 142, 143 (top), 146-47: Paula Goldman. 140 (center and bottom): Richard Andres, Larry Tate, Ron Carraher. 143 (bottom): Squidds & Nunns. 144 (top), 145 (top): Philipp Scholz Rittermann. 152: Joel Meyerowitz, courtesy of *The New Yorker*. 155, 156 (top), 159 (bottom): Roy Porello. 178: © The Museum of Modern Art, New York. 179: Lee Stalsworth. 180-81: John Hallmark Neff. 182: Bill Jacobson Studio, courtesy of The Pace Gallery, New York. 183-84, 186-87: Joel Meyerowitz, courtesy of *The New Yorker*. 208: Roy Porello.

Robert and Adele Irwin, La Jolla, 1993